Delight in the Details

40+ techniques for charming embellishments and accents

Lisa M. Pace

NORTH LIGHT BOOKS
Cincinnati, Ohio
www.mycraftivity.com

 Published by Memory Makers Books, an imprint of F+W Media, Inc., 4700 East Galbraith Road, Cincinnati, Ohio 45236. (800) 289-0963. First edition.

14 13 12 11 10 5 4 3 2 1

Distributed in Canada by Fraser Direct
100 Armstrong Avenue
Georgetown, ON, Canada L7G 5S4
Tel: (905) 877-4411

Distributed in the U.K. and Europe by David & Charles
Brunel House, Newton Abbot, Devon, TQ12 4PU, England
Tel: (+44) 1626 323200, Fax: (+44) 1626 323319
E-mail: postmaster@davidandcharles.co.uk

Distributed in Australia by Capricorn Link
P.O. Box 704, S. Windsor, NSW 2756 Australia
Tel: (02) 4577-3555

Library of Congress Cataloging-in-Publication Data
Pace, Lisa M.
Delight in the details / Lisa M. Pace. -- 1st ed.
p. cm.
Includes bibliographical references and index.
ISBN 978-1-59963-085-4 (pbk. : alk. paper)
1. Paper work. I. Title.
TT870.P24 2010
745.54--dc22

2009025846

Editor: Kristin Boys
Designer: Corrie Schaffeld
Production Coordinator: Greg Nock
Photographers: Christine Polomsky, Al Parrish
Stylist: Jan Nickum

www.fwmedia.com

About the Author

Lisa M. Pace loves all things that sparkle, show dimension and look vintage. Her first memory of creating a project was as a three-year-old sitting at the kitchen table with her mom. From then on she devoted her life to honing skills as a mixed-media artist. Her most recent artistic outlet has been papercrafting. Since 2005, she has had numerous items published in magazines and idea books. In May 2007, Lisa was selected as one of five master scrapbookers in Martha Stewart's scrapbooking contest, and she was chosen as a 2008 Memory Makers Master.

Lisa's success is marked by her ability to rethink and reuse, and her commitment to always add that special embellishment that sets her work apart from others. Lisa currently lives in Frisco, Texas, with her husband and two daughters. She says that the heart of her designs is "in the details."

To learn more about Lisa, visit her at www.lisapace.com.

Metric Conversion Chart

to convert	to	multiply by
Inches	Centimeters	2.54
Centimeters	Inches	0.4
Feet	Centimeters	30.5
Centimeters	Feet	0.03
Yards	Meters	0.9
Meters	Yards	1.1

Dedication

This book is dedicated to all the moms who sit with their little ones while they create masterpieces from finger paint and Play-Doh, just as my mom did with me.

Thanks, Mom. I love you.

Acknowledgments

There is an African Proverb that says, "It takes a village to raise a child." Well, let me tell you, it takes a village to create a book! There are so many people at F+W Media and North Light Books who helped along the way. I know I never could've accomplished this without every one of you. Great big thanks are given to you all.

Thank you to four very special friends. Without you four, I never would have made it through this process. You all accept my quirky artist ways and give more encouragement on a daily basis than some receive in a lifetime.

Caroline, I had no idea the journey I would begin when we became friends. You've given me the courage to reach out and grab many a dream, this book being one of them. I will always be thankful for your friendship.

Jessica, what can I say? You are an awesome friend always accepting my phone calls and e-mails of panic at any time of the day or night. You are always encouraging and somehow manage to keep me focused on today's task instead of looking at all the tasks ahead. Believe me I know this is a huge job.

Lisa, I am so glad you persevered in trying to convince me I would love scrapbooking even when I told you over and over it just wasn't for me. You were right, and I was so very wrong. Thank you so much for being incredibly supportive with all my crazy scrapping ventures all these years.

Wendy, what would I have done without your encouraging e-mails? Always positive, always supportive and always reinforcing that I could and would do this. You never allowed me to think differently.

I thank all of you for your patience, support and encouragement, but most of all, your friendship. I am so glad to call you four my best of friends.

Thank you to Christine Doyle. I will never forget our first chat about creating this book. I'm sure I looked like a deer caught in headlights. Thank you for helping turn a longtime dream into reality.

Thank you to my editor, Kristin Boys. Wow, did you ever have your work cut out when my project landed on your desk! Thank you for always being so supportive, answering all my questions and keeping me on track. You helped turn this book into something I will cherish forever.

Thank you to my fabulous photographer, Christine Polomsky. You were such a wonderful host when I visited your studio. You made my projects look incredible.

Special thanks to Fiskars and iLoveToCreate, a Duncan Enterprises Co., for generously donating all the adhesive I used on the projects in the book.

Thank you to all the wonderful companies who so generously donated their products: Clearsnap; Cocoa Daisy; Cornish Heritage Farms; Fiskars; German Corner LLC; Imagine That! Designs; iLoveToCreate, a Duncan Enterprises Co.; Jenni Bowlin; Kenner Road; Marks Paper Company; Maya Road; Melissa Frances; Little Yellow Bicycle; My Mind's Eye; Paper Tales Inc.; Pebbles Inc., Pink Paislee; Pink Persimmon; Prima Marketing; Ranger; Scor-Pal; Studio 490/Stampers Anonymous; Tim Holtz; Webster's Pages.

Contents

Happy Birthday
Dear Friend

Supplies: Dresden trim, patterned paper (Jenni Bowlin); ink (Clearsnap); pom-pom trim (Maya Road); pearls (Creative Charms); Victorian scraps (Victorian Scrapworks); Misc: thread, twine, Cluny lace, eyelet

INTRODUCTION
Thrill of the Hunt

I love the feeling I get when walking into a thrift store. I never know what I will find stashed on a dusty shelf around the next corner. My heart flutters with excitement as I hunt for treasures to use for storing my tools and supplies as well as unique items to use as embellishments in projects. This is how I envisioned the layout of this book for you. I wanted you to have something a bit unexpected with every turn of the page. On some pages you will find projects like mini albums and banners; on others you will find cards and tags; while on still others you'll discover scrapbook layouts and wall hangings.

Shopping in thrift stores is a favorite pastime; I am always finding a neat old shirt or fabric remnants that I can incorporate into projects. I find lovely buttons, loads of vintage paper and forgotten pieces of jewelry. The best moments are when I come across an old shirt with fabulous pearl or rhinestone buttons, which I can then use for dressing up flowers or rosettes. Buttons adorn almost everything I create! It's these little finds that keep my heritage projects authentic and add to their simple charm of days gone by. Found objects, no matter their state, can always be used in a creation. Even though items may have severely tattered edges or broken pieces, they can be reinvented giving life to a project. Remember, perfection is not always a good thing—faded and tattered adds charm and timeless beauty.

This book, and also my work—with a hodge-podge of vintage goodies, wet media, textures and charming details—resemble the mystique of a thrift store, and that pretty much describes my personality as well. I seem to be all over the place creatively, and I really enjoy the journey of creating. Most of what I've learned has come the hard way through trial and error, but I love to share my tips and techniques so you can cut to the chase of creating! I work with many different media in my projects. This book includes many of my favorites. Of course, I love glitter and all things that sparkle and shine, but I often include fabric and other beautiful textures, along with paint and gloss and dimensional accents.

You should know that you will get glitter on your hands and ink under your fingernails, but that's OK! It will wash off, but the joy of the creative process will remain.

Stickles
Distress

A Delightful Place to Create

As in my projects, it's all about the details in my studio. I wanted to created a work space that felt like a warm and inviting extension of my home, so I incorporated details for storage and display that match the style throughout my house. Because I have always had a love for all things old, no matter their condition or original purpose, vintage items of all kinds make their home in my studio. Since I am limited on space, I not only wanted my studio to be inspirational but also functional. I always look for unique ways to use items such as bowls, luggage, planters and cooking tins for storage. Filled with small embellishments just waiting to adorn a project, muffin tins make any drawer look sweet. All these repurposed objects keep me organized and add unique charm to the space. I also use antique finds such as metal floral frogs to display photos, cards and tags and old canning jars to store flowers and ribbons. I enjoy having these items out in the open as eye candy and inspiration. It is amazing how much product you can store inside even the smallest piece of luggage.

Welcome to my creative space! Come on in and get comfortable.

(Clockwise from top) I found this little wooden shelf all beat up and tattered at a resale shop. I added a coat of black paint and some wax metallic finish to create a nice spot for my supplies. The angel had been all over my house until she found her way into my studio. One day, as I was digging around for certain rhinestone buttons, and it occured to me that it would be nice to display these beautiful gems. So I pinned them on the angel. She sits atop of a piece of luggage where I store additional supplies. At a thrift store I found this milk glass dish that houses a collection of buttons. The dish of buttons reminded me of a little nest, so I set my thrift store bird on top as a pretty accent.

Using my typewriter to create journaling strips is one of my favorite things to do. To keep journaling cohesive with my heritage-themed projects, I like to type in the blank margins of vintage books or on old ledger paper as they already have a faded and distressed look.

I like to organize my glass and pearl buttons in vintage drinking glasses of any shape or size. This way I can see what I have, they look pretty sitting on a shelf and I can keep them handy at my work station.

I use most of the storage items in my scrap space for purposes other than their intended ones. Crystal bowls sitting on a small silver tray and vintage spoons are perfect items to create a glitter station. Salt and pepper shakers are a great way to store glitter, too. Old planters are perfect to hold my most-used self-adhesive pearls and rhinestones. A large milk glass vase holds my favorite scissors.

Minor Details

Where is your studio located?

In my home in Frisco, Texas.

What does your work space look like?

It looks like organized chaos! When I work, especially if I have a deadline, as soon as I finish a project I pick up all the supplies and place them in a pile away from my work station. Then I pull out supplies for another project. This means I end up with piles on the table, on top of books and sadly all around the floor.

What's your favorite vintage find in the space?

It's one that actually I did not find. My mom and I were doing a little antique shopping, and as we were purchasing some items, she asked the clerk if they had any old Underwood typewriters. To my amazement the clerk answered yes, she had one in her car!

Where do you purchase most of your vintage items?

I love to shop in thrift stores for storage items like glassware, muffin tins, old books and planters. This is where I usually end up getting the best price. Antique stores are great for purchasing items such as vintage postcards, ledger paper and pearl buttons. I find pieces of luggage that work great for storage, too.

Because my button collection can be a bit overwhelming, I wanted to sort them by seasonal colors. This way I would have to store only four main button containers. I headed to a thrift store and found four clear stacking salad bowls that worked perfectly. I like to keep items at different heights on the shelves because it makes it easier to see and reach for product. This old scale is perfect for this. Plus, I think it looks so cute!

I have quite a few small embellishments that I like to keep sorted yet close together. I've found old muffin tins work perfectly for this task. If you have more than one of the same style tin, you can stack them for easy storage on shelves. They're also thin enough to place inside drawers.

HOME

Sparkle and Shine

It's no secret that I love all things that glitter. If it sparkles, I must have it! I find a way to incorporate sparkle and shine into all of my projects, whether it's beautiful glass glitter or a vintage rhinestone button. In this chapter you will learn to create your own charming accents that catch the eye. Try just a bit of shimmer such as the glitter brad on page 18 or the hanging jewels on page 26. Or go over the top with vintage-inspired glitz, like the fabulous mica heart on page 22. No matter your level of glitter tolerance, you'll want to give these charming accents a try. You'll see how simple, subtle and not-so-messy glitter can be. And if glitter, rhinestones and all things shimmery excite your creativity, then this chapter is filled with techniques you will dearly love.

Supplies: adhesive; lacquer (iLovetoCreate); chipboard (Maya Road); decorative scissors (Fiskars); glitter (Art Institute); ink (Clearsnap); patterned paper (Foof-a-la); Misc: lace, tray, vintage button, flowers, seam binding, acrylic paint

Glitter Glue Edges

I love finding items on their way to the trash—like a beat-up photo easel I came across—and turning them into something beautiful. And, of course, a little shimmer makes everything look fabulous! After removing the easel's faux wood matting and painting it with a silver leafing pen, I covered the frame with silver glass glitter. The easel is dressed in flocked patterned paper and accented with a corsage from vintage flowers similar to the type my mom (shown in the photo with my dad) would have worn. Glitter glue is an easy addition to any project; use it to accent adorable paper banners and edge other pretty details, like my crepe paper rosettes (see more on page 64).

Supplies: decorative scissors (Fiskars); glass glitter (German Corner LLC); patterned paper (Making Memories, Little Yellow Bicycle); punch (Fiskars); ribbon (Novtex, Offray); silver leafing pen (Krylon); vintage berry pick, flowers, leaves (Paper Tales Inc.); Misc: crepe paper, rhinestones, easel, vintage buttons, corsage pins

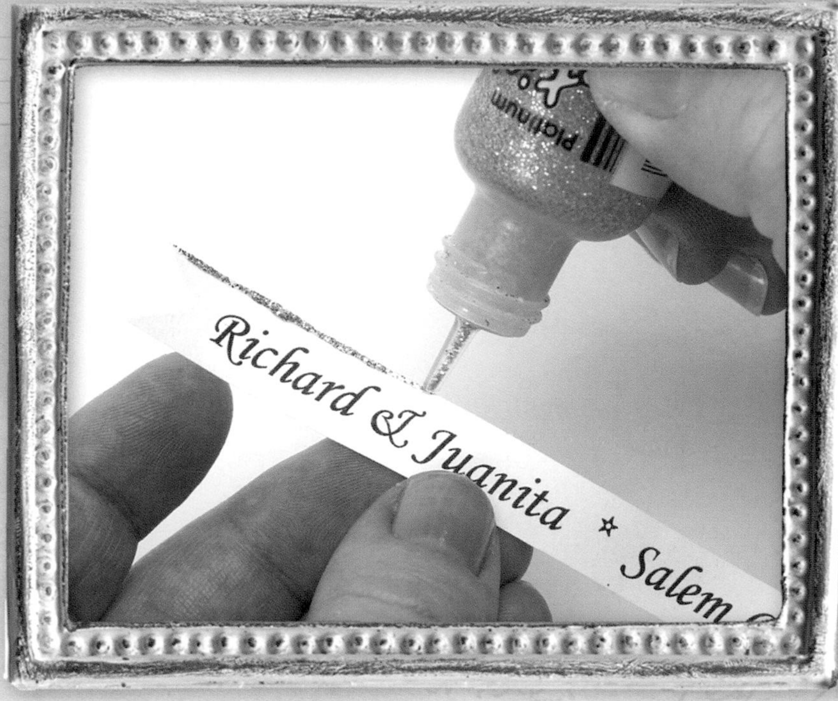

What You'll Need

glitter glue, embellishment

Apply glitter glue

Gently squeeze the bottle of glitter glue along the edge of your embellishment and allow it to dry. Be careful not to stick your fingers in the glue before it dries!

More Delightful Details

Try edging your entire piece with glitter glue as I did on this Christmas ornament. Give your little banner a vintage feel by typing a sentiment onto a scrap of an old book page margin. Then add dimension using layers and curling the mini banner with your fingernail before attaching it to your piece.

Supplies: bells (Jo-Ann); journaling coaster, scroll frame (Maya Road); glass glitter (German Corner LLC); glitter glue (Ranger); ink (Clearsnap); Misc: jump ring, twine, buttons, chandelier piece, vintage sheet music, acrylic paint, rhinestone, crackle medium

Shimmery Pattern

I never feel a piece is complete without a bit of glitter, but sometimes (just sometimes!) something subtle will do. On these kinds of projects, crystal coarse glitter is the perfect choice. Not sure where to apply the shine? Just follow your pattern! This super sweet pink polka-dot paper is perfectly accented with a bit of shimmery detail. For this card I wanted a lot of different textures. To accompany the glitter, I added soft details like lace, velvet blossoms and tulle. The button tops everything off to make a card that's cute as a ... you know.

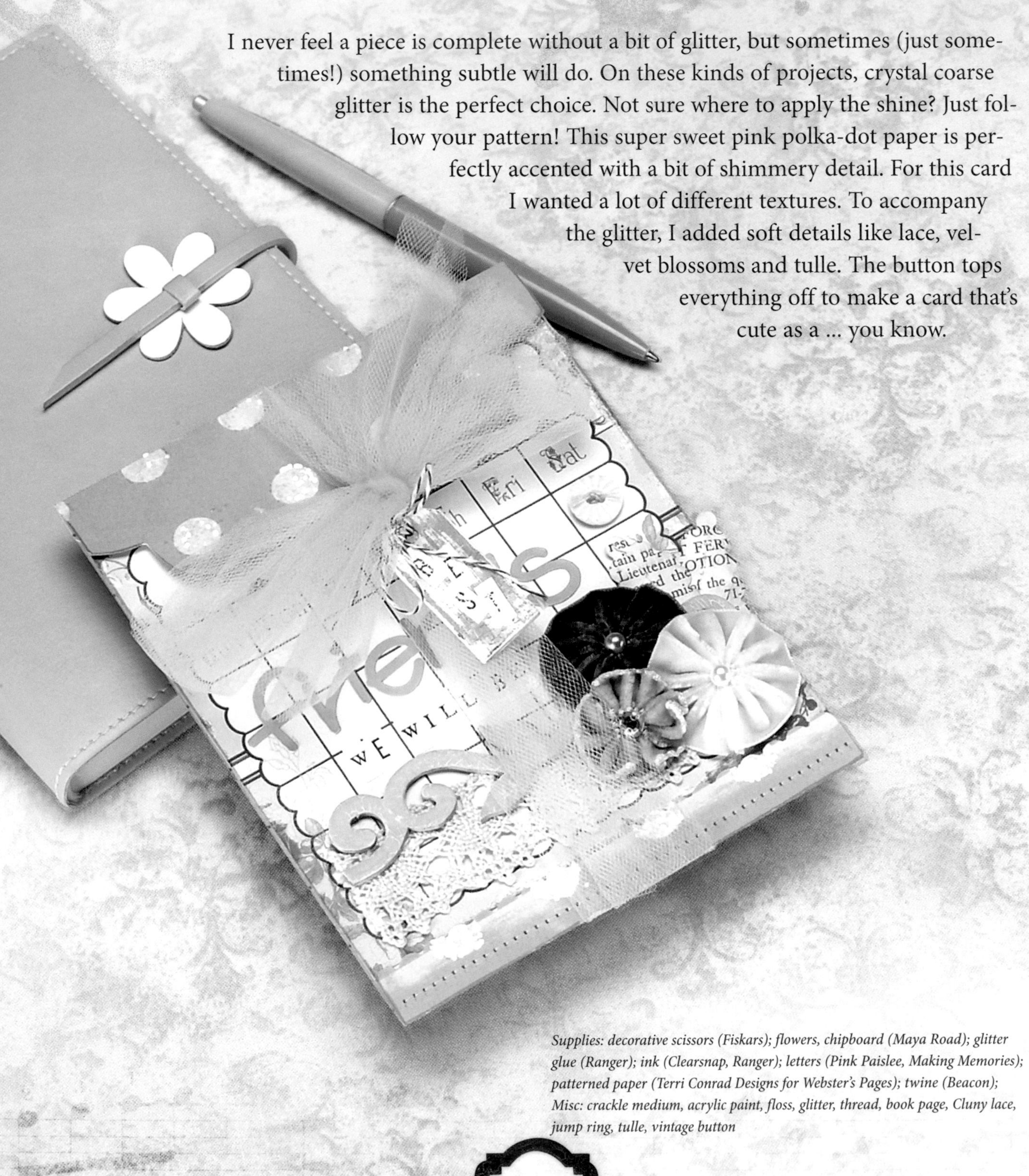

Supplies: decorative scissors (Fiskars); flowers, chipboard (Maya Road); glitter glue (Ranger); ink (Clearsnap, Ranger); letters (Pink Paislee, Making Memories); patterned paper (Terri Conrad Designs for Webster's Pages); twine (Beacon); Misc: crackle medium, acrylic paint, floss, glitter, thread, book page, Cluny lace, jump ring, tulle, vintage button

What You'll Need

patterned paper, gloss medium intended for paper (Paper Glaze), glitter

1. Apply gloss medium

Apply gloss medium intended for paper to various spots in the pattern on your patterned paper. (It is important to use a gloss like Paper Glaze as it will not buckle your paper.)

2. Add glitter

Sprinkle glitter on top of the wet gloss medium.

3. Remove excess glitter

Using your finger, gently press glitter into the gloss medium. Then tap off the excess glitter, and let it dry.

More Delightful Details

Polka dot isn't the only pattern that can shine. Try accenting circles—like the brightly hued ones on this happy card—spirals, flowers, stripes or butterflies. I used glitter glue to accent the flower here, but any glitter will work. Chipboard dressed with crackle medium provides a delightful contrast to shiny patterned paper.

Supplies: buttons (K&Co.); scallop frames (Maya Road); die (Sizzix); glitter glue (Ranger); ink (Clearsnap); patterned paper (My Mind's Eye); rub-ons (Melissa Frances); Misc: floss, thread, acrylic paint, crackle medium, card

Glitter Brad

No detail is too small to make shine! A simple way to up a project's sparkle is to glitter your own brads. Plus, this way you can always match the color to any project you have in mind. On this pretty card, I accented a distressed paper flower with a brad dressed in tinsel-cut glitter, which complements the shimmery chipboard swirls. The glitter provides a nice contrast to the distressed look of the paper and the stamped bingo image, which I created using Tim Holtz Distress Powders—my favorites!

Supplies: chipboard, pins, stamp (Maya Road); decorative scissors (Fiskars); embossing powder, ink (Ranger); patterned paper (Terri Conrad Designs for Webster's Pages); pearls (Michaels); punch (EK Success); ribbon (Jo-Ann); misc: brad, floss, glitter, acrylic paint, punch, vintage buttons

What You'll Need

tweezers, brad, paintbrush, acrylic paint (same color as glitter), dimensional gloss medium, glitter

1. Paint brad

Holding your brad with tweezers, paint the top of the brad using the acrylic paint.

2. Apply gloss medium

Carefully apply dimensional gloss medium to the top of the painted brad.

3. Dip brad in glitter

Dip the brad into the bottle of glitter. Gently press the top of the glittered brad with your finger to set the glitter. Tap the brad to get rid of excess glitter. Let it dry.

Shiny Alphas

Like an unpainted canvas, plain chipboard letters are a natural choice for dressing up—especially with glitter. Sitting atop a berry sprig, *hope* shines on this butterfly hanging, with the help of chipboard adorned in crystal fine glitter. A few velvet pleats, some pinwheel blossoms, a white seam-binding bow and a sprinkling of rhinestones complete this unique and cheerful hanging. Adding glitter to your letters is simple, but following important steps will ensure they get a full coverage of sparkly goodness.

Supplies: chipboard shapes, flowers (Maya Road); gems (Offray); ink (Ranger); lace (The Paper Studio); patterned paper (K&Co.); Misc: glitter, acrylic paint, thread, canvas, berry spray, pom-pom trim, vintage seam binding

What You'll Need

plain chipboard letters, ink or paint (same color as glitter), dimensional gloss medium, tweezers, glitter

1. Ink letter

Ink or paint the chipboard letter and allow it to dry.

2. Apply dimensional gloss medium

Cover the letter with a layer of dimensional gloss medium. Use tweezers to pick up the wet letter and place it on scrap paper.

3. Cover with glitter

Generously cover your letter with glitter. (This will ensure all the edges are covered.) Using your finger, gently press the glitter into the gloss medium.

4. Remove excess glitter

Pick up the letter with tweezers, and gently tap off the excess glitter. Allow the medium to dry.

More Delightful Details

My nephew is all boy, hence the title of this layout. Brittain loves fishing and hunting and is a huge University of Texas fan. I thought it would be nice to have a layout showcasing his favorite all-boy moments. But that didn't mean I couldn't add some glitter! Bronze works well for a masculine page. On this layout, I created the title by dressing up plain chipboard letters and placing a black mother of pearl button at each end.

Supplies: letters (Maya Road, Making Memories); patterned paper (My Mind's Eye); Misc: floss, glitter, thread, vintage buttons

Mica Heart

Love really shines on this adorable card. I used silver wire sprays adorned with rhinestones to give the illusion of wind blowing as the mica-covered chipboard heart flies away. Perfect for Valentine's Day, anniversaries or any time you want to share the love, this little "Love Is in the Air" card provides a whimsical, romantic gesture. The card centers around the chipboard heart, adorned with a jeweler's tag and baker's twine. Vintage-transfer wings help the heart fly. To craft a similar card, start with soft pastel shades of patterned paper and add warm tones of brown satin ribbon, cream lace and velvet rickrack.

Supplies: chipboard (Maya Road); decorative scissors (Fiskars); gems (Offray); ink (Clearsnap); mica powder (Greg Markim); patterned paper (Prima, Making Memories); rhinestone buckle (Gartner Studios); ribbon, rickrack (May Arts); vintage transfer (Melissa Frances); Misc: acrylic paint, lace, thread, card

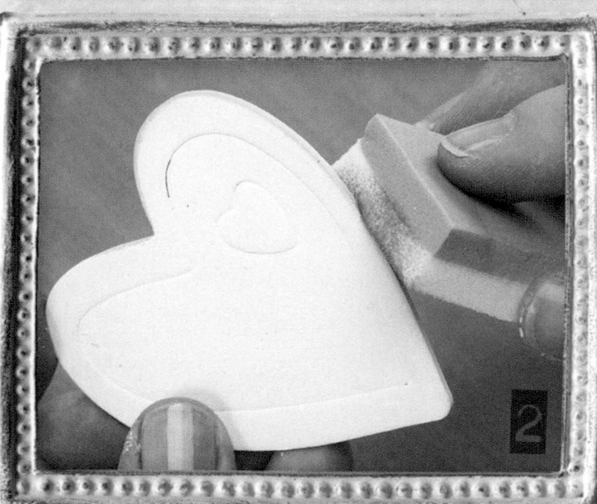

What You'll Need

chipboard heart, ivory acrylic paint, chalk ink, dimensional gloss medium, mica powder, jeweler's tag, rub-on word, baker's twine

1. Paint chipboard

Paint the chipboard heart using acrylic paint. Allow the paint to dry.

2. Ink edges

Apply chalk ink to the edges of the heart.

3. Add dimensional gloss medium

Fill the heart with dimensional gloss medium.

4. Sprinkle mica powder on heart

While the gloss medium is still wet, generously sprinkle mica powder over the entire heart. Allow the gloss medium to dry.

(continued)

5. Add rub-on to tag

While the gloss medium is drying, add a rub-on word to the jeweler's tag.

6. Wrap with twine

Wrap baker's twine a few times around the heart and secure it with a knot. Then attach the jeweler's tag.

All That Glitters

There are so many beautiful types of glitter and similar materials to make projects shine. The ones in this photo are my favorites. I like to make little glitter stations of my most-used glitters, containing the glitter in crystal bowls found at thrift stores. I apply the glitter to my projects with old vintage spoons.

Clockwise from left: fine iridescent glitter, medium-grit silver glass glitter, copper tinsel cut glitter, clear glass shards, glitter glue, sparkling mica powder, coarse glitter, glass beads

I think every birthday should have a little sparkle, which is just what I wanted for this tag. I decided to cover this chipboard frame using silver glass glitter as I love the heavier texture and brighter sparkle, perfect for a frame. You apply glass glitter in the same manner as I applied mica dust to the heart embellishment. Glass glitter comes in a variety of colors as does mica powder.

Supplies: chipboard frame, crushed velvet (Maya Road); felt (C.P.E.); glitter (German Corner LLC); patterned paper (Jenni Bowlin); rub-ons (Melissa Frances); Misc: floss, twine, buttons, flocked flowers, tulle, vintage seam binding, rhinestones, acrylic paint, eyelet

Hanging Jewels

I love to decorate for the holidays and can always find a spot for a festive banner. Banners have so much potential. You can wrap them around a holiday tree, adorn a window, stretch them across the top of a hutch or hang them from a shelf. Last year, I wanted to touch up my cabinet with a little joy, a pop of color and some shimmer, so I created this banner, adding simple hanging jewels for holiday lights to catch. Glittery snowflakes and subtle gold beads add a nice finishing touch.

Supplies: beads (Hobby Lobby); crystals (Heidi Swapp); chipboard letters (Maya Road); frames (Ranger); glass glitter (German Corner LLC); liquid embossing (Plaid); patterned paper (Melissa Frances); rickrack, banner (Maya Road); snowflakes (Target); twine (Beacon); Misc: acrylic paint, tulle

Every Last Detail

When looking for holiday decorations, think beyond the obvious. The snowflakes used in this banner are meant to be tree ornaments. I clipped off the hangers, added more glitter and used them as the base for the letters.

What You'll Need

paper piercer, jump rings, large crystal beads

1. Poke hole

Poke a hole near the bottom of your project using the paper piercer.

2. Attach bead

Insert the jump ring into the hole. Then thread the bead onto the jump ring and close the jump ring. Add additional beads as desired.

More Delightful Details

This chipboard coaster was initially meant to be an arrow, but I thought it would make an adorable birdhouse. The entrance to the birdhouse is a scallop frame I dressed with patterned paper, German glass glitter and silver gems. I made the bling extra special using a chandelier accent created from a piece of broken necklace. For added durability, I strung the gems from an eyelet-enforced hole.

Supplies: chipboard arrow, scallop frame (Maya Road); decorative scissors (Fiskars); felt (C.P.E.); glass glitter (German Corner LLC); ink (Clearsnap); patterned paper (Jenni Bowlin); pearl gems (The Paper Studio); silver gems (Michaels); vintage flower (Paper Tales Inc.); Misc: glitter, pen, twine, chandelier piece, jump rings, vintage necklace, eyelet

Wire Spray

This photo of my daughter Terri was taken one day right after shc came home from work. I felt it showcased her character and life at that moment perfectly. I documented her personality with a few words assembled using tiny letter stickers. I used glittered chipboard numbers to record Terri's age, and I framed the photo with rhinestones, which is a quick and easy way to bring focus directly to a photo. But all that bling called for other accents with only a hint of shine. If you want to add a splash of color with a little bit of shimmer, create delicate wire sprays with transparent beads. They add whimsy to a layout, and the butterflies here appear to fly on by.

Supplies: bling borders (Advantus); butterfly charms (Maya Road); chipboard numbers (Advantus); flower (Prima); glitter glue (Ranger); leaves (Prima); letters, pom-pom trim (Making Memories); patterned paper (My Mind's Eye); punch (EK Success); trim (Maya Road); Misc: eyelets, thread, beads, Cluny lace, office tags, tags, vintage seam binding, wire

Every Last Detail

I've found it easiest to use a hot glue gun to secure wire sprays to a project.

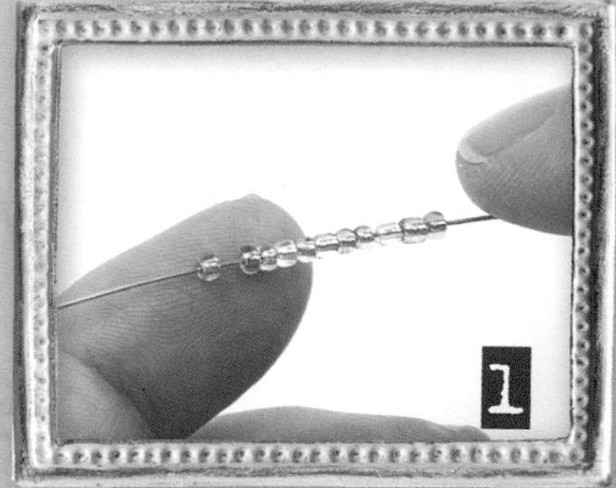

What You'll Need

24-gauge wire, wire cutters, transparent seed beads, butterfly charm or other charm beads

1. String beads

Using wire cutters, cut your wire to the desired length. String about ten seed beads on one end of the wire, leaving about 1" (3cm) of empty wire at the end.

2. Secure loop

Bend the beaded wire to create a loop. Twist the wire together to secure the loop.

3. Add charm

Thread three more beads onto the wire. Then add a butterfly charm.

4. Bend more loops

Thread about ten more beads onto the wire. Bend the wire to create another loop and twist together to secure. Repeat the steps to create more loops, and add more charms as desired.

More Delightful Details

There are different forms of wire sprays you make, such as the one I used here. I crafted a spray using just a single charm and wire, and one using a simple button. To make these sprays, fold pieces of wire into upside-down "V"s in different heights. Slip a bead or button onto a "V," then hold the bead at the point of the "V," and twist the wire down to the end.

Supplies: beads (Blue Moon); button, bird coaster, scroll, blossoms, heart charms (Maya Road); crystal (Heidi Swapp); eyelet (Jo-Ann); glass glitter (German Corner LLC); ink (Clearsnap); jeweler's tag (American Tag Co.); patterned paper (My Mind's Eye); pearl (Creative Charms); stamp (S.E.I.); Misc: twine, chandelier piece, vintage rosary beads, acrylic paint, wire

JOY

Paint and Ink

If you like having dried paint on your hands, ink under your nails and glue on your fingers, well, you're going to love the techniques in this chapter! Paint and ink are messy, but altering chipboard and paper using wet media is a simple way to introduce charming detail and make an impact on finished projects. Start with quick and easy techniques—like the chalk ink accents on page 32 and the alpha doodles on page 40. Then move on to more creative techniques like the paper mosaic on page 48, where faux tiles look like delicate china pieces. Playing with alcohol ink is always fun, and the technique shared on page 36 is simple yet dramatic. You'll also try out texture paste and crackle medium, dimensional gloss and more. So get out those baby wipes and paper towels because we are going to get messy!

Supplies: bling borders (Heidi Swapp); book binding tape, patterned paper, ribbon (Making Memories); button (Junkitz); album, chipboard letters, snowflakes, rickrack, rub-ons, chipboard keychain, flowers, jewel, journaling sheers (Maya Road); decorative scissors (Fiskars); glass glitter (German Corner LLC); holly (Jo-Ann); ink (Clearsnap); bells (Darice); twine (Beacon); Misc: crackle medium, floss, acrylic paint, rhinestones, tags, thread, cord, vintage seam binding

Chalk Ink Accents

Monochromatic color schemes are great for ensuring that projects have a cohesive look. But sometimes it makes for papers that blend a little too well, causing your project to appear flat. It's the delightfully simple details that come to the rescue in cases like these. To solve the problem, just accent part of a pattern using pearl chalk ink. The added color and hint of shine provide dimension that will make a project pop. I highlighted the flowers and sweet bird on this layout that features a very young me.

Supplies: alphabet (Advantus); patterned paper (Jenni Bowlin Studio); chalk ink (Pebbles Inc.); stickers, letters (Making Memories); Misc: photo corners, thread, gold rhinestones

What You'll Need

chalk ink (two colors), chalk ink applicator, patterned paper with picture (such as a bird)

1. Add color to image

Apply one color to the picture using a chalk ink applicator. Here I'm filling in the body of a bird with yellow ink.

2. Apply darker shade

Apply a darker shade of chalk ink to highlight different areas of the picture. Here orange ink accents the bird's belly, adding dimension.

More Delightful Details

I love this butterfly stamp, but the antennae create quite a challenge when cutting them out. So I stamped the butterfly directly on the tag, then I stamped another butterfly on ledger paper and cut it out, skipping the antennae. The image on the tag provided me with antennae, and the version on the paper was able to fold up and fly. Using chalk inks for color, I accented all the butterflies to make them pop.

Supplies: chalk (Pebbles Inc.); decorative scissors (Fiskars); ink, glitter glue (Ranger); patterned paper (Jenni Bowlin); pearl gems (The Paper Studio); stamp (Studio 490/Stamper's Anonymous); buttons (Paper Tales); vintage newspaper (Kenner Road); Misc: floss, thread, office tag, rhinestone

Antique Frame

I have always loved this photo of my grandparents' home. To me it is the perfect place, with a wonderful front porch where we watched cars drive by while we laughed and snapped peas. To display these wonderful memories, I crafted a wall hanging using patterned papers, ribbon and trim that reminded me of items inside the old home. The wood grain ribbon reminds me of the grandfather clock, and the music notes remind me of the piano on which my mom practiced her lessons. The flowers recall the blooms in my grandmother's sun-porch, while the crystals recall the door and dresser drawer knobs. To top off the heritage photo display, I wanted to add a vintage frame. All I had was a new white one, but a simple distressing technique using wax metallic finish gave it that worn look.

Supplies: alphabet (Advantus); patterned paper (Jenni Bowlin Studio); chalk ink (Pebbles Inc.); stickers, letters (Making Memories); Misc: photo corners, thread, gold rhinestones

What You'll Need

frame with ornate details, fluid chalk ink (two neutral colors like brown and tan), gold wax metallic finish (Rub 'n Buff), paper towel

1. Add ink to frame

Apply chalk ink to the raised portions of the frame, starting with the lighter ink color first. Then apply a small amount of the darker shade of ink in the same manner.

2. Apply wax finish

Using your finger, apply the wax metallic finish to the raised portions of the frame (over the inked areas). Wipe off excess wax with a paper towel.

More Delightful Details

The lid of this box incorporates several layers of different techniques using crackle paint, glitter, crepe paper, vintage ephemera and inks. The layered details make the perfect base for my vintage-inspired floral embellishment to sit atop. I distressed the resin flowers using two shades of brown ink along with wax metallic finish. Tiny pearls and glitter glue add lovely detail.

Supplies: box (Jo-Ann); crepe paper ribbon (Jenni Bowlin); decorative scissors (Fiskars); Dresden trim (German Corner LLC); frame (Maya Road); ink (Clearsnap, Ranger); pearls (Mark Richards, The Paper Studio); vintage embellishment (Melissa Frances); Misc: acrylic paint, glitter, book page, medallion, vintage sheet music

Alcohol Ink Stamp Resist

The starting point for this piece came from the name of the ink colors I used for the background technique—Caramel, Ginger and Latte—which reminded me of time spent at my grandparents' house. So I built the piece using their house as inspiration. The alcohol ink resist makes for a soft, worn background, perfect for a heritage piece. Sitting atop the background detail is chipboard that resembles the fence surrounding my grandmother's garden. The velvet blossom, leaves and embossed chipboard vine represent Grammy's love of gardening. I created the little fairy using a photo of my mom as a child. To top it all off, vintage rosary beads accented with vintage seam binding and baker's twine make a delicate hanger.

Supplies: acrylic tile, grunge material (Tim Holtz); alcohol ink, glitter glue, archival ink, dimensional gloss medium (Ranger); chalk (Pebbles Inc.); chandelier pieces (Michaels); chipboard, flower (Maya Road); Dresden trim (German Plaza); embossing folder (Provo Craft); gilding medium (USArtQuest); leaves (Paper Tales); patterned paper (Making Memories, Webster's Pages); pearl (Michaels); stamps (Fiskars); Misc: brads, eyelets, vintage beads, vintage seam binding

What You'll Need

transparent acrylic tile, alcohol ink (three similar colors), alcohol ink applicator, archival ink, corner stamp, paper towel, dimensional gloss medium, cardstock, scissors

1. Ink acrylic tile

Add all three alcohol inks to the same applicator. Dab the applicator on the acrylic tile until the tile is covered in ink. Twist the applicator after each dab (waiting five seconds in between each application); this will provide a mottled look.

2. Stamp image on tile

Ink your stamp with the archival ink. Stamp on the alcohol-inked side of the acrylic tile.

3. Remove inked image

Wipe off the inked image using a clean, dry paper towel.

4. Attach to cardstock

Cover the alcohol-inked side of the tile with dimensional gloss medium. Set the gloss side facedown onto cardstock. Move the tile in a circular motion so you spread the gloss medium around to clear out any air bubbles. Once it's dry, cut off the excess cardstock.

More Delightful Details

Even without the stamp resist, alcohol ink makes for interesting details on a project like this simple plaque. I cut a flower accent from a transparent sheet and from a page of sheet music. After layering the transparent flower over its patterned twin (using vellum tape), I applied a mix of alcohol inks over the top.

Supplies: alcohol ink, glitter glue, ink (Ranger); buttons (Melissa Frances); letters, chipboard heart (Maya Road); die (Sizzix); stencil sheet (Plaid); buttons (Paper Tales); Misc: adhesive, floss, fabric, vintage sheet music

Faux Porcelain Flowers

As a young girl, when I saw ceramic flowers in the floral section at craft stores, I was always confused. I just could not understand why anyone would chose them when they could have the real thing. But when planning this Mother's Day project, I found myself wishing I had some of those very same flowers—indestructible and perfect for a keepsake box. I never despair when I don't have something on hand. I created my own porcelain-looking blooms using a flower setting agent and regular silk flowers. I love how they turned out!

Every Last Detail

You can use a flower setting agent on silk ribbon and fabrics, too.

Supplies: bling borders (Heidi Swapp); book binding tape (Making Memories); flower setting agent (Plaid); glaze (Design Master); ink (Clearsnap); mini album, velvet, suitcase (Maya Road); patterned paper (Making Memories, Melissa Frances); punch (Fiskars); twine (Beacon); vintage embellishment (Melissa Frances); Misc: crackle medium, glitter, acrylic paint, lace, silk flowers, tulle, vintage flowers, vintage seam binding

What You'll Need

silk flower, paintbrush, flower setting agent (Petal Porcelain), glossy spray sealer

1. Brush on setting agent

Brush the setting agent on the flower, completely covering each petal. Be sure to get in all the tight areas and the front and back of the petals. Set aside to dry. Let the flowers dry overnight.

2. Spray with sealer

Once the flower has completely dried, spray it with the glossy sealer in a well-ventilated area. Spray 2–3 coats of sealer, allowing it to dry between sprays.

More Delightful Details

Silk roses are lovely, but you can transform any silk flower into a nice faux porcelain accent. This Mother's Day box gets cheery with bright pink daisies and zinnias. I created the lace ruffle that frames the porcelain bouquet using the same method that I use to fashion a crepe paper ruffle (see page 68). A glitter-accented banner makes a nice finishing touch.

Supplies: box (Maya Road); clear glaze (Design Master); distress crackle paint, glitter glue (Ranger); flower setting agent (Plaid); ink (Clearsnap); paint, patterned paper, letters (Making Memories); Misc: thread, Cluny lace, silk flowers

Alpha Doodles

I have wonderful friends who are so sweet to me and my family, so I thought "So Sweet" would make an excellent title for a card. Keeping on the sweet theme, I used glitter glue to accent sweet polka dots, created a scallop trim using decorative scissors and accented each corner with three self adhesive pearls. Using brightly colored patterned paper keeps up the card's cheery theme. I created the little rosette embellishment by stacking several punched circles with different edges on top of a crepe paper rosette. To complete the rosette I inked an "s" using chalk inks and added doodles using a white opaque pen.

Supplies: decorative scissors (Fiskars); glitter glue (Ranger); ink (Clearsnap, Ranger); letters (Maya Road, Webster's Pages); patterned paper (Webster's Pages); pearls (Melissa Frances); pen (Ranger); punch (EK Success, Fiskars); Misc: book page, thread, card, crepe paper

What You'll Need

plain chipboard letter, ink, opaque pen

1. Ink letter

Ink the chipboard letter. Allow it to dry.

2. Draw doodles

Using an opaque pen, accent the outer edge with lines and dots.

More Delightful Details

Kelly and Belinda
welcome
Isabella Kate
7 lbs. 11 oz.
May 23, 2007
19 inches
12:25 p.m.
sweetest
dreams

Sweet doodles are a delightful addition to the letters in the title of this adorable baby layout. In addition, the softness of the inked letters complements the tulle shown in the photos and also used on the layout.

Supplies: bling borders (Heidi Swapp); chipboard, flower (Maya Road); decorative scissors (Fiskars); glitter glue (Ranger); ink (Clearsnap, Ranger); patterned paper (Crate Paper, Prima); ribbon (May Arts); pins (Heidi Grace); stickers (Making Memories); Misc: fabric, tulle, thread

Textured Letters

It's never too late to scrap old photos! I took theses photos of my daughters in 2004, and just recently added them to a page, highlighting their colors with bright, snow-themed paper. A great project is in the details, right? With accents of glitter and glass that give them an ice-capped look, the letters really make this wintry page stand out. Machine stitching and scalloped edges complete the pretty project.

Supplies: chipboard letters (Maya Road); decorative scissors (Fiskars); diamond dust (FloraCraft); die-cuts, glaze, patterned paper (My Mind's Eye); glitter glue, gloss medium (Ranger); Misc: acrylic paint, thread

What You'll Need

plain chipboard letter, acrylic paint, paintbrush, glitter glaze, dimensional gloss medium, clear glass shards, container, spoon

1. Paint letter

Paint the chipboard letter with acrylic paint. Allow the paint to dry.

2. Add glitter glaze

Brush glitter glaze over the painted chipboard and allow it to dry.

3. Apply gloss medium

Add dimensional gloss medium to a few spots around the letter.

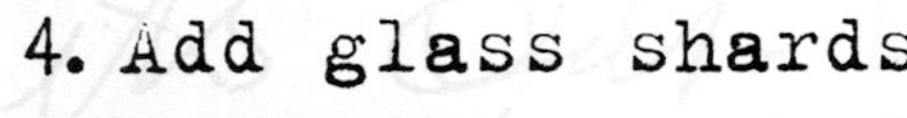

4. Add glass shards

Hold the chipboard letter over a container of clear glass shards. (Note: You can use clear glitter, if you prefer.) Use a spoon to sprinkle the glass shards over the areas with gloss medium. Remember that you are working with finely cut glass, so carefully pat down the glass shards using your finger and tap off any excess.

Distressed Alphas

To build on the wintry theme of this page about my grandfather shoveling snow and pulling huge icicles off the side of the house after a bad winter in 1978—I added lots of ice-cold details: blue metallic trees, rhinestones, glittery snowflakes and white pom-poms that resemble ice and snow. I also altered chipboard alphas using blue and white paints and crackle medium. Crackle medium is a staple in country home decor; why not use it in projects, too? I wanted to give each letter and number the look of ice, and the crackles create a wonderful feel. With the aged and textured look it provides, crackle medium works well for any vintage-themed project.

Supplies: chipboard (Maya Road); die-cut (Ellison); liquid embossing (Plaid); punch (Fiskars); stickers (Making Memories); Misc: crackle medium, acrylic paint, glitter, photo corners, rhinestones, thread, pom-pom trim

What You'll Need

plain chipboard letters, acrylic paint (two colors), brush, crackle medium

1. Paint the first color

Paint the chipboard letter with acrylic paint. Use the color that you want the cracks to be. Let it dry.

2. Apply crackle medium

Generously brush on crackle medium to cover the painted letter. Allow it to dry.

3. Brush on top color

Apply the second paint color. Be sure to apply just one coat and avoid painting over an area more than once, otherwise it will not crack properly.

More Delightful Details

I found this toile tissue paper in a little gift shop, and as soon as I saw it, I instantly knew it would be saved for a future project. Not too long after that, I stumbled upon this frame that needed a pick-me-up. I altered chipboard letters using crackle medium, and now they are the star of the piece. This perfectly pretty wall hanging goes to show that crackle medium works well in adding detail to any kind of project.

Supplies: bling borders (Heidi Swapp), chipboard (Maya Road), decoupage medium (iLoveToCreate), patterned paper (Making Memories), ribbon (May Arts); Misc: crackle medium, acrylic paint, frame, pom-pom trim, tissue paper, vintage button, vintage flowers, vintage seam binding, brads

Cracked Chipboard

Just as crackle medium provides an icy look for winter projects, crackle paint provides a wonderful, rough texture, perfect for dressing natural shapes like twigs, petals and leaves. Crackle paint like Distress Crackle Paint from Tim Holtz is a simple one-step method to produce cracked paint. To create more depth in the cracks, you can apply a coordinating ink. So, in just a few easy steps, you can say a beautiful hello to a friend, with two little tweeting birds sitting atop a branch.

Supplies: chipboard, rub-ons (Maya Road); crackle paint, glitter glue (Ranger); decorative scissors (Fiskars); die-cut (Sizzix); felt (C.P. E.); ink (Clearsnap); patterned paper (My Mind's Eye); pearls (Creative Charms); Misc: card, floss, thread, book page, vintage sheet music

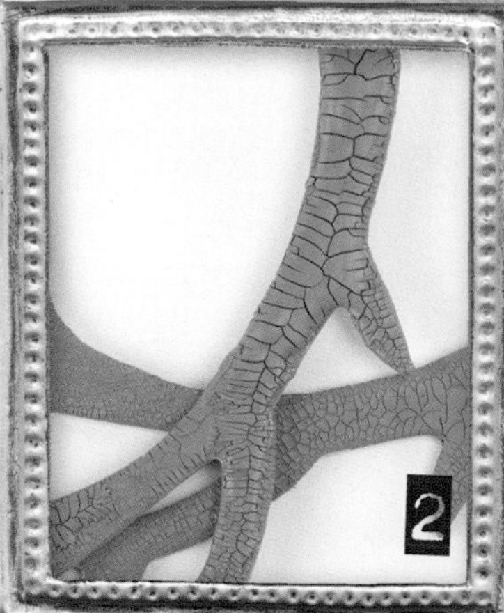

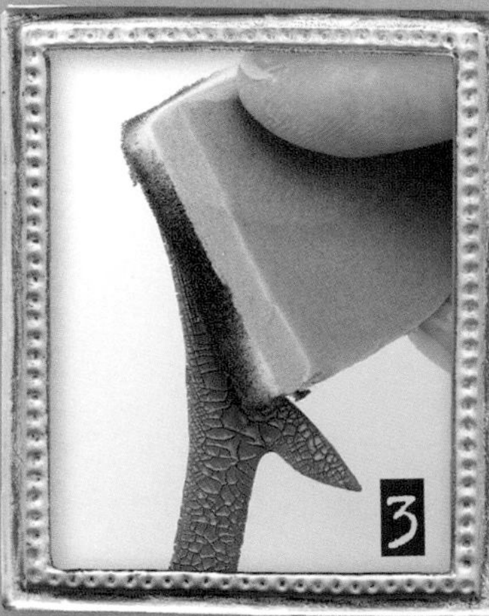

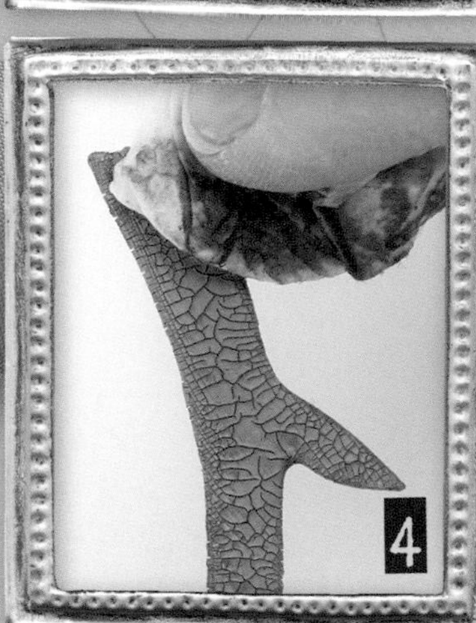

What You'll Need

chipboard embellishment, crackle paint (Distress Crackle Paint), distressing ink (Distress Ink), damp cloth

1. Apply crackle paint

Apply a medium to thick coat of distress paint to the chipboard piece. If the coat is too thin, the paint won't crack well, so apply paint liberally.

2. Allow paint to dry

Allow the paint to dry. (Once the paint starts to crackle you can speed the drying using a heat gun.) Notice how the thickness of the paint affects the size of the cracks. The branch on top has a thick coat, while the one underneath has a medium coat.

3. Ink over cracks

Apply an ink color darker than your paint color to the chipboard. Be sure to get the ink into the cracks.

4. Wipe off ink

Wipe off the ink using a damp cloth.

More Delightful Details

As you can see, crackles provide wonderful texture for flower accents. This flower embellishment is easy to create. To do so, cut three identical flowers from a thick material like chipboard or Tim Holtz Grungeboard. Cut two blooms off their stems, and toss one of the stems. Paint the three flower blooms with crackle paint, and ink the two remaining stems. Add glitter to the flower that's still intact (bloom and stem) and one of the other blooms. Then layer the pieces: the stem on the bottom, the intact flower over that, then the bloom without glitter, and six petals cut from the bloom with glitter. Add a pretty vintage button over the top.

Supplies: crackle paint, glitter glue, grunge material, ink (Ranger); die-cut (Sizzix); jewels (Creative Charms); filigree (Little Yellow Bicycle); stamp (Cornish Heritage Farms); Misc: punch, twine, eyelet, office tag, vintage seam binding

Paper Mosaic

Many gardens have at least one mosaic stepping stone that leads you to dew-covered leaves on a misty morning with a butterfly fluttering among the flowers. This image inspired me to create the pages for this garden-themed album. The simple mosaic technique allows you to fake the look of a ceramic tile mosaic, and provides pretty patterns for a project. I used faux grout medium, but acrylic paint does the job nearly as well. To complete the album, I added glittery polka dots on the spine's ribbon to resemble that of the morning dew.

Every Last Detail

Make sure you keep a straight pin handy to pop any air bubbles that form in the dimensional gloss medium.

Supplies: album, chipboard, rub-ons (Maya Road); bling borders (Heidi Swapp); book binding, lace (Making Memories); decorative scissors (Fiskars); crackle paint, faux mosaic kit, glitter glue (Ranger); ink (Clearsnap); fibers (BasicGrey); flower (Prima); patterned paper (Making Memories, Webster's Pages); punch (EK Success); Misc: butterflies, flowers, lace, pearls, ribbon, tags, acrylic paint

What You'll Need

patterned paper scraps, scissors, large chipboard piece, paintbrush, faux grout medium (Faux Mosaic) or white acrylic paint, tweezers, decoupauge medium, dimensional gloss medium

1. Cut paper into pieces

Cut scraps of patterned paper into small pieces.

2. Brush on faux grout

Brush chipboard piece with faux grout medium or white paint. Cover the chipboard completely with a thick layer of medium (using two coats if needed). Allow it to dry.

3. Arrange mosaic

Arrange paper on chipboard until you are satisfied. Then carefully lift each piece using tweezers, brush decoupage medium on the back and re-place it.

4. Apply gloss medium

Brush a coat of decoupage medium over the entire mosaic and allow it to dry. Then add a coat of dimensional gloss medium to each paper piece. Be sure not to get gloss medium onto the "grout." Set aside to dry.

More Delightful Details

I used faux grout medium to create the paper mosaic on the mini album. The grit of the faux grout medium is perfect for an outdoor garden theme. I substituted white paint for the grout medium on this little butterfly hanging, achieving a similar look.

Supplies: decoupage medium, gloss medium (iLoveToCreate); beads (Blue Moon); chandelier crystals (Heidi Swapp); butterfly (Maya Road); patterned paper (My Mind's Eye); Misc: book page, jump rings, pom-pom trim, rosary beads, vintage seam binding, vintage flowers, wire, eyelets, acrylic paint

Texture Paste Design

The inspiration behind the cover of this mini album was an old dresser I saw while browsing an antique store. I loved its raised resin design and the aged and faded look of the paint. Fortunately, I was able to re-create the look for this album's cover using texture paste and pastel-colored paints. I accented the album with vintage rhinestone buttons to give it some old-fashioned Hollywood glamour. Filled with thoughtful quotes, this simple album is a lovely way to honor the simpler times of days gone by.

QUOtEs
Too much of a good thing can be wonderful.
Mae West
You are so much sunshine in every square inch.
Walt Whitman
Shoot for the moon. Even if you miss, you will land among the stars.
Anonymous

Supplies: decorative scissors (Fiskars); glitter glue (Ranger); ink (Clearsnap); letters, patterned paper (Making Memories); mini album, pins (Maya Road); stencil (Complements); texture paste (Delta); Misc: acrylic paint, thread, vintage rhinestone buttons

What You'll Need

stencil with floral design, texture paste (any color), palette knife, removable tape (optional), acrylic paint (neutral color for the background and two colors for the design), paintbrush, neutral-colored fluid chalk ink, water, thin bristled brush, transparent glitter glue, vintage button, strong adhesive (like hot glue)

1. Spread paste

Place the stencil over the background surface. Using a palette knife, spread the texture paste over the stencil making sure to keep the stencil in place. (You can secure it with removable tape if needed.)

2. Remove stencil

Once the stencil design is filled with texture paste, gently remove it from the background. Allow the texture paste to dry completely.

3. Paint background

Paint the entire background, including the design, using the neutral-colored acrylic paint.

(continued)

4. Apply chalk ink to background

Apply a blend of neutral-colored chalk inks to the painted background. Apply the ink in light circular motions to create a shaded effect.

5. Paint design

Add about 1–2 teaspoons (5–10 ml.) of water to thin the other two colors of acrylic paint. Using a thin bristled brush, apply paint to color the textured design. Allow the paint to dry.

6. Add glitter glue

Accent the textured design using transparent glitter glue.

7. Attach vintage buttons

Attach a vintage button to each flower center using a strong adhesive like hot glue.

Every Last Detail

Don't overlook a product just because the color isn't right. I used purple texture paste for this project (it was on clearance) because the acrylic paint would cover it up. Also, if you purchase white texture paint, you can tint it with small amounts of acrylic paint.

Getting Messy

There was a time I feared using any type of wet media. Paints, inks, glazes—they all scared me. I was so worried about messing up a project that I just stayed away. What a big creative loss that turned out to be! If you fear wet media like I did, now is the time to stop. If you want to start out slow, try applying inks to accent the edges of patterned papers or chipboard. I use a stamp pad foam for inking the edges of my projects and a blending tool for larger areas like album covers or chipboard letters.

Acrylic paints can be applied straight out of the bottle or placed on a tray mixed with a few teaspoons of water to create a unique color wash for subtle color accents. You can apply paint with a foam or bristle brush. I prefer bristle brushes as I feel I waste too much paint with a foam brush. I also like to use Adirondack Acrylic Paint Dabbers (by Ranger). These have a sponge tip applicator on the top of the bottle which makes them convenient and basically mess free—perfect for wet media newbies!

Another fun wet media I like to use is glitter glaze. This specialty glaze is perfect for those that dislike the mess of loose glitter but still like an iridescent look. This specialty glaze can be applied to the top of dried ink or paint. Dye-based and iridescent mists are another wet media that bring life to projects. You can spray these onto chipboard embellishments instead of using paint or ink. You can also use them with stencils or masks.

Remember, perfection is overrated… don't fear making a mistake because you will miss out on lots of fun!

More Delightful Details

To me, birthdays are all things sweet and sparkly, and what better embellishment to use for this project but a chipboard cupcake? I used texture paste to give the appearance of icing on top. To achieve a similar look, all you have to do is squeeze a small amount of paste onto chipboard and spread it using a spatula—just as you would real frosting! To give the liner of my cupcake a more realistic look, I added vertical stitches with my sewing machine. To pull the piece together, I painted the scallop base the same color as the icing and applied coarse glitter.

Supplies: chipboard (Maya Road); decorative scissors (Fiskars); glitter glue (Ranger); patterned paper (Pink Paislee); pearls (Michaels); texture paste (Delta); vintage transfers (Melissa Frances); Misc: eyelet, glitter, acrylic paint, rhinestones, thread, office tags, pom-pom trim

For You

Pattern and Texture

Paper is, of course, the foundation of any papercrafting project, but with all those lovely patterns, it makes for fabulous details as well. Add fabric and trim to the mix, and you'll have wonderful texture, too. Stitching and cutting are perfect ways to create charming accents with basic tools, but they certainly make a project anything but basic. Pattern and texture will help you achieve an elegant heirloom feel with little effort or mess. In this chapter, you'll try your hand at a crepe paper rosette (page 64) and a fabulous felt bloom (page 80) that are perfect embellishments for layouts, cards and tags. I'll also show you how simple machine stitches add a cozy, homemade feel—no experience required! On page 78, you'll finally find a reason to stock up on fabric remnants, and on page 90 discover a unique way to create your own embroidery patterns from stamps you have on hand.

Supplies: decorative scissors (Fiskars); felt (C.P.E.); ribbon (Magic Scraps); ink (Clearsnap); stamp (Studio 490/Stampers Anonymous); Misc: floss, pearls, thread, Cluny lace, trim, vintage sheet music, card

Decorative Edges

Creating a set of mini cards is a great way to use up your paper scraps. To start my own, I created a basic design that was easy to duplicate on multiple cards. The cards feature a delicate scallop border that frames a simple sentiment. Decorative-edge scissors make creating pretty edges easy, and knowing the right technique helps achieve perfect corners—well-done projects are all in the details! Accents like glitter glue, punched scallop circles, buttons, stitching and rhinestones dress up the cute little greetings. Give a set to a friend as a gift or just create a bunch to add to your own stash.

Supplies: buttons (Melissa Frances); decorative scissors (Fiskars); flocking powder (Stampendous); ink, glitter glue (Ranger); patterned paper (Little Yellow Bicycle); punch (Fiskars, Marvy); stamp (Cornish Heritage Farms); Misc: embroidery floss, thread

What You'll Need

patterned paper, decorative scissors with small scallops

1. Cut edge of paper

Starting at one corner, carefully cut the edge using decorative scissors with small scallops.

2. Cut corner

Flip the paper over so that the previously cut section is on the bottom and the straight edge to be cut is to your right. Match up your existing scallop with the curve on the scissors and cut.

More Delightful Details

You can create tiny eyelet edges like those on the edges of this layout by poking holes in your scallops using a paper piercer. To embellish this sweet layout I added pom-pom trim, rhinestones, buttons and yummy glitter chipboard letters. Keeping with the theme of the patterned paper's cross-stitch design, I cross-stitched on the sides of the photo using floss.

Supplies: bling borders (Advantus); buttons (Autumn Leaves); letters (American Crafts, Maya Road, Making Memories); decorative scissors (Fiskars); patterned paper (Cosmo Cricket); Misc: floss, thread, twine, glitter, pom-pom trim, acrylic paint

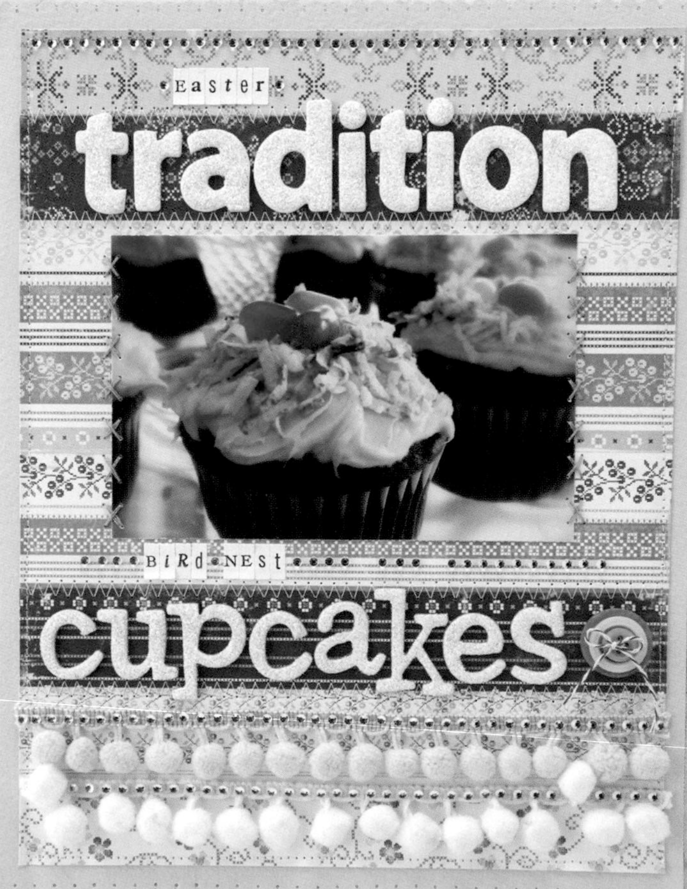

Eyelet Border

Family makes me think of a quilt. Each quilt is pieced together using different shades and patterns of fabric, then stitched together with love. Quilts provide warmth and comfort and that feeling is exactly what inspired me to create this layout. I chose several different patterned papers with warm tones, pieced them together and stitched along the edges of each piece just as one would a quilt. To finish the layout, I crafted a simple eyelet border and accented the page with ribbon and lace.

Supplies: berry spray (Michaels); buttons (Maya Road); chipboard (Heidi Swapp); decorative scissors (Fiskars); ink (Clearsnap); patterned paper (Melissa Frances); ribbon (Prima); rub-ons (Maya Road); Misc: lace, pom-pom trim, seam binding, floss, office tag, photo corners, thread

Every Last Detail

To give a slight distressed look to your paper edges once you have sewn them together, carefully run your fingernail along each edge until you get the look you like.

What You'll Need

patterned paper, decorative scissors with large scallops, small hole punch

1. Cut edge of paper

Staying close to the edge of your paper, cut the paper using decorative scissors with large scallops. If it is hard for you to cut a straight line, turn your paper over, trace a line using a pencil and straightedge and cut along that.

2. Punch holes

Punch a hole in the center of each scallop.

More Delightful Details

Creating your own eyelet circle is easy—really! All you need is a dinner plate. I'm sure you have several different sizes in your cupboard right now. Select the appropriately sized plate and trace it onto the back of your paper. Once you try this technique, you will never look at a dish—or anything around the house—the same way again.

Supplies: decorative scissors (Fiskars); alphabet stickers, lace, (Making Memories); bling borders (Advantus); buttons (Maya Road); ink (Clearsnap); patterned paper (SEI); glitter glue (Ranger); Misc: punch, thread, twine, book page, acrylic paint

Miniature Banner

To create a dimensional foundation for the tiny banner declaring love, I covered a chipboard page from a heart album with patterned paper and trimmed it in scallop rickrack. Wanting more texture, I used my machine to sew straight and zigzag stitches and I accented the papers using glitter glue. Then I applied the finishing touch with vintage architectural details altered with paint and ink. Sentiments are, of course, the most important things on a card, so after I completed this card, I wanted to create a unique way to display the words. Creating a mini banner is a great way to not only add a whimsical element but also to add dimension.

Supplies: chipboard, trim, flowers (Maya Road); decorative scissors (Fiskars); glitter glue (Ranger); ink (Clearsnap); patterned paper (Terri Conrad Designs for Webster's Pages); pearls (Michaels); twine (Beacon); vintage details (Melissa Frances); Misc: card, acrylic paint, thread

What You'll Need

computer and printer or typewriter, cardstock, scissors or trimmer, decorative scissors with pinking edge, baker's twine, liquid adhesive

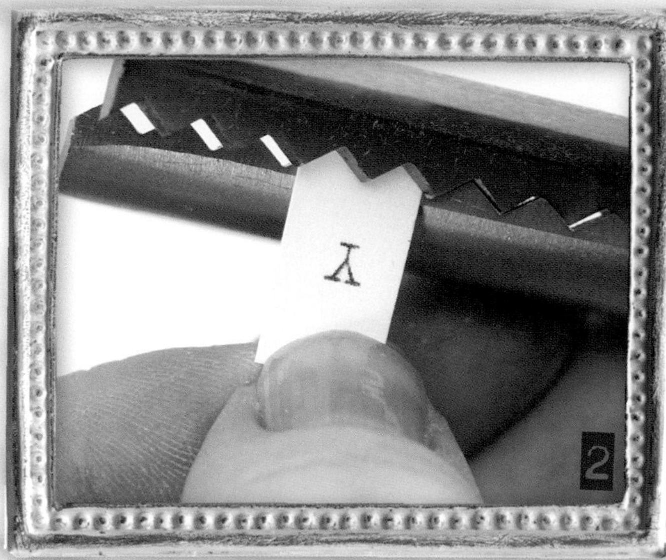

1. Print and cut sentiment

Type your sentiment, triple spacing between each letter. Print the sentiment on cardstock if you are using a computer. Cut out each letter strip, leaving space above and below the letter.

2. Cut decorative edge

Trim the bottom edge of each letter using the decorative scissors. Place the point of a zigzag in the center to create an edge with two "V"s.

3. Attach letters to twine

Cut a piece of baker's twine to the desired length. (The length will depend on the length of your sentiment.) Apply a dot of liquid adhesive to the top back part of a letter, then fold the top end over the baker's twine and hold in place until it's dry. Continue until all the letters are attached to the twine.

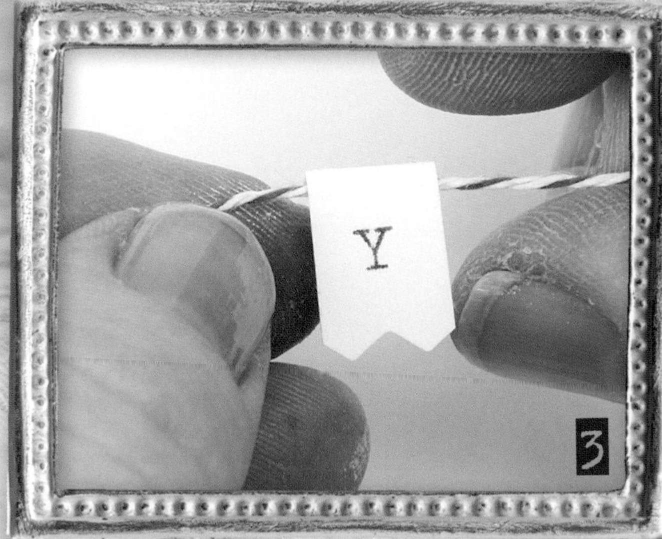

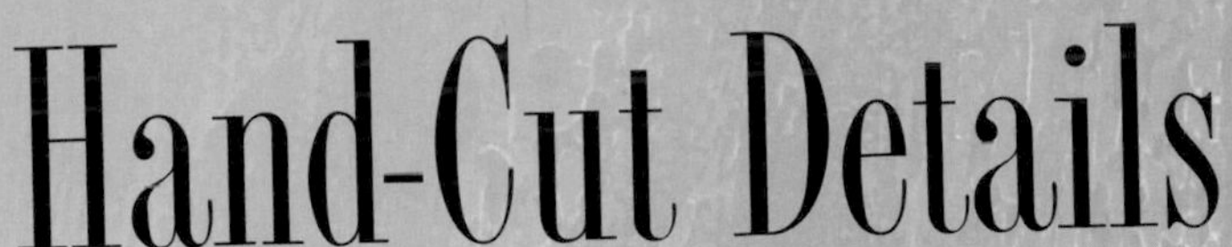

Hand-Cut Details

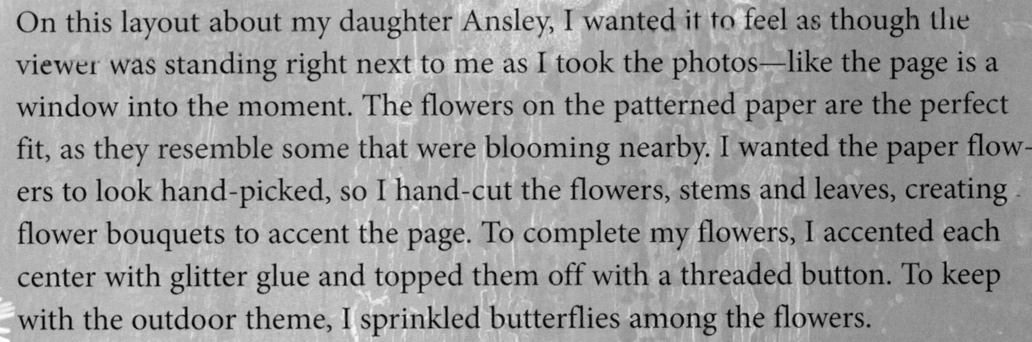

On this layout about my daughter Ansley, I wanted it to feel as though the viewer was standing right next to me as I took the photos—like the page is a window into the moment. The flowers on the patterned paper are the perfect fit, as they resemble some that were blooming nearby. I wanted the paper flowers to look hand-picked, so I hand-cut the flowers, stems and leaves, creating flower bouquets to accent the page. To complete my flowers, I accented each center with glitter glue and topped them off with a threaded button. To keep with the outdoor theme, I sprinkled butterflies among the flowers.

Supplies: buttons (My Mind's Eye); chipboard letters, pom-pom trim (Maya Road); decorative scissors (Fiskars); glitter glaze, glitter glue (Ranger); ink (Clearsnap); patterned paper (Pink Paislee); pearls (Mark Richards); Misc: floss, punch, thread, photo corners, acrylic paint

What You'll Need

floral patterned paper, craft knife, button, floss, adhesive dot, butterfly punch, tweezers, small self-adhesive pearls

1. Cut out pattern

Using a craft knife, cut out a flower from the patterned paper.

2. Tie thread to button

Tie a few strands of floss in a bow through the buttonholes. Attach the button to the cut-out flower using an adhesive dot.

3. Add pearls to butterfly

Punch (or cut) a small butterfly out of the second pattern. Fold the butterfly in half to give the wings dimension. Use tweezers to add the pearls to the center of the butterfly.

More Delightful Details

As simple as they are, buttons—hand tied with thread—add such sweet detail to a project. I created the base of this card using several pieces of an old sewing pattern cut with pinking scissors and topped with ivory felt. These squares are cut from remnant pieces of fabric that were going to be tossed. Talk about a lucky find! I punched circles out of sewing pattern, which I topped with a collection of ivory vintage buttons. I finished off the card with an old millinery flower and a simple sentiment.

Supplies: decorative scissors (Fiskars); felt (C.P.E.); jeweler's tag (American Tag Co.); Misc: floss, punch, buttons, sewing pattern, vintage flower, card

Crepe Paper Rosette

As a child, I always loved getting a birthday card from my grandmother, and she happens to be the inspiration behind this card. I mix and matched several patterned papers to give the card the feel of an old quilt. Gram was a wonderful quilter, so I stitched a checkered pattern to replicate quilting in her honor. The star of the card is a delicate crepe paper rosette accented with sparkle. What says "Happy Birthday" more than crepe paper? Buttons, seam binding and baker's twine complete the vintage chic theme.

Supplies: buttons (Melissa Frances); decorative scissors (Fiskars); glitter glue (Ranger); ink (Clearsnap); patterned paper (K&Co.); twine (Beacon); vintage transfers (Melissa Frances); Misc: leaves, vintage seam binding, vintage sheet music, office tag, rhinestone, thread

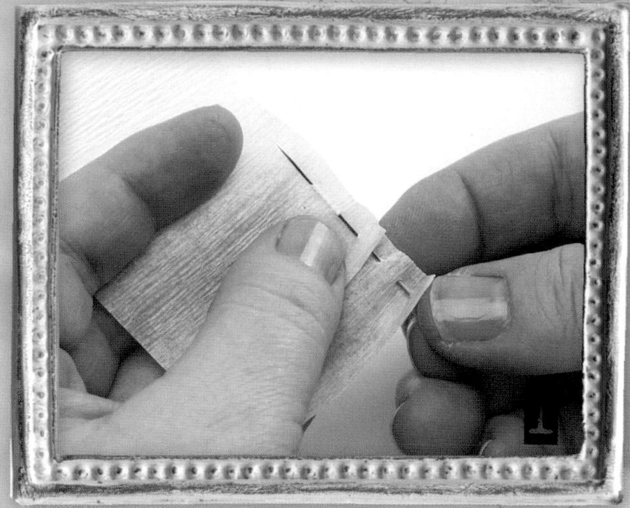

What You'll Need

crepe paper, needle, floss, scissors, vintage button, strong liquid adhesive (like Tacky Glue or a hot glue gun), glitter glue

1. Start running stitch

Cut a strip of crepe paper about 12" (30cm) long. Thread your needle with a few strands of floss. Then start a running stitch at one end of the crepe paper. Use a gentle hand so you don't tear the crepe paper.

2. Gather crepe paper

Continue the running stitch to the other end of the strip. As you stitch, gather the crepe paper onto the needle.

(continued)

More Delightful Details

Crepe paper rosettes are so lovely—and so versatile! Use them as flowers on a project or as a foundation for an embellishment. The rosette is just one of many layers that adorn this any-occasion card. Behind it sits a scalloped circle dressed with the tiniest of pearls. On top is a smaller scalloped circle punched from an old book. The rosette acts as a unique frame for the circle. I topped the stack with a crackled heart and tiny paper bow accented with—what else?—platinum glitter glue.

Supplies: chipboard heart (Maya Road); glitter glue (Ranger); ink (Clearsnap); patterned paper (Jenni Bowlin); gems (Michaels); punch (Fiskars); Misc: floss, thread, book page, buttons, acrylic paint, crackle medium, card, crepe paper

3. Tie ends

Remove the needle from the floss. Then pull the crepe paper ends together to form a circle. Tie the ends of the floss in a knot.

4. Cut rosette

Fold up the rosette and trim the ends until you get the diameter you want.

5. Attach button

Open up your rosette and attach a button to the center using strong liquid adhesive.

6. Add glitter glue

Accent the edges with glitter glue.

Every Last Detail

You can use decorative scissors to cut the ends of your rosette for even more pretty detail.

More Delightful Details

I most often dress up crepe paper rosettes with rhinestone buttons, but they aren't the only option. This little tag, which features children's book-inspired stamps assembled to look like paper dolls, called for something simple and down-to-earth. A button trimmed with baker's twine provides the perfect accent to complete the look.

Supplies: ink (Clearsnap, Tsukineko); markers (Imagination International); patterned paper (Making Memories); pearls (Michaels); pom-pom trim (Maya Road); stamp (Pink Persimmon); glitter glue (Ranger); Misc: floss, thread, twine, book page, Cluny lace, button, office tag, crepe paper, eyelet

Tools of the Trade

Cutting decorative edges to paper and fabric is one of the simplest ways to add detail to a project. And using decorative scissors and punches is the quickest way to get those fancy edges.

There are certain punches and scissors I like to keep close at hand because they work for so many techniques. My staple decorative punches and scissors always have a pinking or scalloped edge. Fiskars' squeeze punches with the scallop edges are my favorites because they are easy to use and come in oval, circle, square and heart shapes. It's handy to have matching shapes in different sizes, like a set of small and large ovals. You can use the punched pieces individually, or place the smaller piece on top of the larger piece to create a wonderful accent. There really are so many uses for punched shapes!

Decorative scissors come in a variety of shapes as well, but large and small scallops and a pinking edge are must-haves. It's also helpful to have a pair of fabric pinking shears. They tend to be sturdy and sharp, and cut chipboard well. You can find these scissors in any sewing or craft store.

More Delightful Details

Sometimes a gift's packaging is more exciting to receive than the gift! I created this delightful gift card holder from felt, ribbons, pearls and vintage sheet music. I accented the layers with a pretty lace bloom. This flower is simple to create—you simply use the same process used to make a crepe paper rosette. All you need is lace, a needle and some floss. Accent the center using a rhinestone button, and you'll have a beautiful embellishment for your package.

Supplies: decorative scissors (Fiskars); distress powder, embossing ink (Ranger); felt (C.P.E.); moire ribbon (EK Success); pearls (Michaels, The Paper Studio); ribbon (The Paper Studio); scallop rickrack (Maya Road); stamp (Cornish Heritage Farms); Misc: floss, leaf trim, pink trim, tag, vintage rhinestone button, vintage sheet music, eyelet

Ruffle Frame

When I saw this patterned paper, it reminded me of wallpaper found in a nursery. I decided to create a layout that resembled a wall showcasing a sweet first-day-home photo. I created delicate ruffles from crepe paper to frame the photo along with a square of patterned paper. I accented each flower in the patterned paper using glitter glue and embellished the faux stitching with hand stitching. To create the "hanger" for the photo, I cut a strip of ribbon, adhered it vertically to the layout and topped it off with a pretty bow.

Every Last Detail

Create pretty accents by cutting thin strips of ribbon with sharp decorative scissors.

Supplies: decorative scissors (Fiskars); die-cut felt (Prima); glitter glue (Ranger); letters (Making Memories); patterned paper (Melissa Frances); pearls (Mark Richards); ribbon (EK Success); Misc: crepe paper, floss, thread

What You'll Need

scissors, cardboard sheet, patterned paper, adhesive, die-cut paper, crepe paper, needle, floss, dry adhesive, photo

1. Layer cardboard with paper

Cut a piece of cardboard 6" (15cm) square. Cut a piece of patterned paper to the same size and adhere it to the cardboard. (Sew a straight-stitch border around the paper before attaching, if desired.) Layer a 6" (15cm) square piece of die-cut paper or felt on top of the patterned paper.

2. Cut and fold crepe paper

Cut a strip of crepe paper about 24" (60cm) long. (To get the correct length for other sizes, measure the perimeter of the photo and multiply that amount by two.) Fold your cut piece of crepe paper almost in half lengthwise (the edge of the bottom layer should peek out from under the top layer).

(continued)

More Delightful Details

There's nothing that says a ruffle can only frame a photo—or even that it has to be square. I sandwiched a narrow crepe paper ruffle between two chipboard hearts dressed in sheet music. Instead of accenting the crepe paper with glitter, as I would with a rosette, I accented the hearts. I wanted a thicker glittered edge than glitter glue provides so I used medium-grit German glass glitter, held on by thick liquid glue.

Supplies: chipboard heart (Maya Road); punch, decorative scissors (Fiskars); crepe paper ribbon (Jenni Bowlin); glass glitter (German Corner LLC); flowers (Paper Tales Inc.); Misc: floss, twine, trim, vintage sheet music

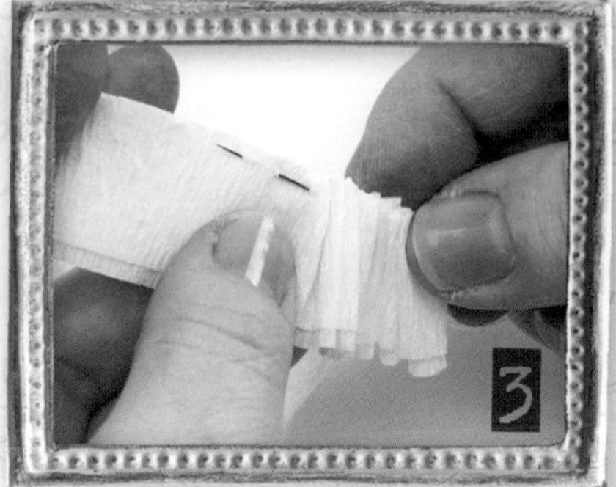

3. Sew a running stitch

Thread a needle with a few strands of floss. Sew a running stitch along the folded edge of the crepe paper, gathering the crepe paper as you stitch.

4. Complete ruffle

Continue your running stitch from one end of the crepe paper to the other. Remove the needle, then adjust the crepe paper until the ruffles are spread evenly along the floss.

5. Attach ruffle to cardboard

Cut a second piece of cardboard 3" (8cm) square. Add dry adhesive to the back of the cardboard along the edges, and attach the crepe paper ruffle.

6. Attach photo

Cut your photo 3" (8cm) square. Turn over the cardboard and attach your photo to the top. Finally, layer the ruffle-framed photo over the piece you created in step 1.

More Delightful Details

Simple yet sweet. That's what I think when I see this card. A simple crepe paper ruffle makes a sweet border. To create a crepe paper border, gather a length of crepe paper using a running stitch. Instead of folding the crepe paper in half first and stitching along the edge, keep the crepe paper unfolded and stitch down the center. Top with velvet trim and soft accents for added texture.

Supplies: velvet, blossom (Maya Road); glitter glue (Ranger); patterned paper (Jenni Bowlin); punch (Fiskars); vintage leaves (Paper Tales Inc.); Misc: thread, card, crepe paper

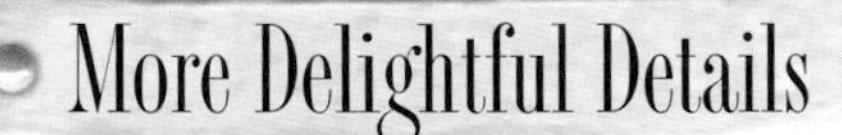

More Delightful Details

Try colored crepe paper to give a project pizzazz! I used pretty pink paper for the mini album's ruffle frame, adding glitter to make it shine. The album filled with photos of simple pleasures sits inside an adorable house built from vintage bingo cards. The door is framed in another crepe paper ruffle cut with pinking scissors for a different look.

Supplies: bird's nest (Hobby Lobby); bling borders (Heidi Swapp); door knob (7gypsies); frame (Melissa Frances); glitter glaze (Li'l Davis); ink (Clearsnap); patterned paper (Webster's Pages); pearls (Mark Richards); rickrack (Maya Road); rub-on (Daisy D's); Misc: crepe paper, pom-pom trim, vintage bingo cards, vintage ledger paper, thread

Gathered Ribbon Border

Handmade tags are a delightful special touch for a gift package. A handmade tag amongst the piles of holiday gifts is especially sweet to receive. You can create a tag quickly using coordinating patterned papers, ribbons and embellishments. I made this one extra-special with a gathered ribbon trim. You can transform nearly any piece of ribbon into a lovely accent or border for a project. (Stay away from sheer ribbon, though, as the glue will seep through.) I used shiny red and gold to trim this holiday tag, but, of course, any color will do.

Supplies: ink (Clearsnap); patterned paper, ribbon (Making Memories); glitter glue (Ranger); tag (DMD Industries); rickrack, flower (Maya Road); Misc: crepe paper, eyelet, floss

What You'll Need

ribbon, fabric glue

1. Add glue and fold

Attach one end of your ribbon to your tag using fabric glue. On top of the ribbon place a small amount of glue, then fold the ribbon over approximately ¼" (6mm) and hold it in place.

2. Fold length of ribbon

Place another small amount of adhesive on top of the fold you just created. Fold the ribbon again as you did in step 1. Continue until you achieve your desired length of ribbon.

More Delightful Details

The inspiration behind this project is the quote, "A kind word is like a spring day." To enhance the spring theme, I made a die-cut flower using felt and tulle-like paper. To keep the piece light and airy I substituted crepe paper for ribbon for the gathered accent. During spring there is always a butterfly fluttering by, so I punched a butterfly and accented it with tiny pearls.

Supplies: bingo card, chipboard button, crepe paper ribbon, patterned paper, rub-ons (Jenni Bowlin); buttons (Melissa Frances); scroll, rickrack (Maya Road); die-cut (Sizzix); glitter glue (Ranger); felt (C.P.E.); ink (Clearsnap, Ranger); pearls (Michaels); Misc: floss, punch, thread, twine, button, Cluny lace, specialty paper, vintage cabochon

Faux Bow

Vintage rhinestone buttons are a wonderful way to accent a heritage project. They are easy to find online and are usually sold in sets. On this layout about my grandmother and namesake (my middle name is Marie), I accented the center of a fancy velvet bow with rhinestones for a formal look; velvet and rhinestones are a perfect pairing. But don't worry if you're not great at tying bows—you can go faux! And if you aren't one for a lot of sparkle, you can add just a few gems.

Texie
Marie
circa
1962
My grandmother and namesake, Texie Marie Cox was born April 8, 1908 in Doddridge County, West Virginia.

Supplies: bling borders, chipboard letters (Advantus); decorative scissors (Fiskars); flower, ribbon (Maya Road); letters (Making Memories); leaves (Paper Tales); patterned paper (Close to My Heart); Misc: floss, eyelet, thread, rhinestone button

What You'll Need

ribbon, scissors, fabric glue, button

1. Cut ribbon

Cut four pieces of ribbon: one the width of your project, one ¾ the width of your project, and two ⅔ the width. Adhere the longest piece of ribbon to the background using fabric glue.

2. Cut ends of ribbon

Cut a "V"-shaped notch on both ends of the next longest piece of ribbon. Do the same with one of the shortest lengths of ribbon.

3. Attach notched ribbon

Adhere the two pieces of ribbon with notched ends over the top of the longest piece of ribbon. Attach the longer ribbon first, and center both pieces.

4. Create bow

Fold the remaining piece of ribbon in thirds and attach each end to the center with fabric glue. This will create the "bow" with two loops.

5. Attach bow and button

Attach the bow to the top, center of the ribbon stack. Add a rhinestone button to the center of the bow.

Every Last Detail

To prevent ends of ribbon from fraying, apply a small drop of liquid seam sealant (like Dritz's Fray Check) to the cut areas. You can also use liquid seam sealant to keep the ends of fabric swatches and handmade flowers or other fabric embellishments from fraying.

Perfect Bow

Each year, my daughters and I look forward to baking our special holiday cookies. Once finished, we keep a few for ourselves and give the rest to family and friends. This simple gesture was the inspiration behind this layout. I used vintage metal cookie cutters as templates for the background paper behind my photos, title and journaling. Then I dressed the layout with a metal-rimmed tag and a big red bow, just as we do when packaging our cookies to give as gifts. Sweet faux bows are great for projects, but sometimes you want the real thing to (literally!) tie it all together.

christmas cookies
Every Christmas Terri, Ansley and I always look forward
to baking our favorite holiday cookies.
Chewies, Red Velvet Kisses and Pecan Sandies
For you
december 25th

Supplies: decorative scissors (Fiskars); ink (Clearsnap, Ranger); patterned paper (My Mind's Eye); stamp (Cornish Heritage Farms, Hampton Art); Misc: glitter, punch, thread, metal-rimmed tag, ribbon, acrylic paint

What You'll Need

ribbon

1. Make two loops

Find the middle of the ribbon and create two loops on either side.

2. Fold loops

Fold the loop on the right over the left and pull it through.

3. Pull tight

Pull the knot tight, and adjust the loops so that they are even.

More Delightful Details

If a big red bow isn't your style, this technique can help you create a perfect bow with any ribbon, such as this thin ivory trim. To complement the sheen of the ribbon, I edged the patterned paper with golden glitter glue. This gives the background a bit more definition and helps the layers to stand out.

Supplies: glitter glue (Ranger); ink (Clearsnap); letters (Making Memories); patterned paper, vintage embellishment (Melissa Frances); pearl gems (Mark Richards); wax metallic finish (Amaco); Misc: thread, twine, office tag, vintage seam binding, eyelet

Fabric Flower

I love to dig through the remnant bin at the fabric store. You never know what you are going to find, and you can pick up some great fabric pieces for minimal cost. You can use these swatches to create your own unique floral accents just as I did when I made this card. Upholstery fabric is my favorite for this technique, as it has a nice texture, and fabric stiffener makes the flower pop. If you don't have trims that match your fabric finds, take a little ink and tint the trim until you get the shade you want. Top off a rough and textured bloom with some bling for contrast, as I did here.

Supplies: spray fabric stiffener (iLoveToCreate); brad (Making Memories); glitter glue (Ranger); ink (Clearsnap, Ranger); patterned paper (Terri Conrad Designs for Webster's Pages); stamp (Cornish Heritage Farms); trim (Maya Road); velvet leaves (Prima Marketing Inc.); Misc: fabric, rhinestones, card, glitter

What You'll Need

fabric, fabric pen, sharp scissors, fabric stiffener, Crop-A-Dile, brad

1. Cut fabric circles

Draw five circles in varying sizes on the back of the piece of fabric using a fabric pen. Circles should vary about ¼" (6mm) in diameter. I used different bottles of glitter and glue as templates. Cut out your circles. You can give the flowers a decorative edge using scallop scissors, if desired.

2. Spray with fabric stiffener

Spray your fabric circles with a good coating of fabric stiffener. Crinkle them in your hand, and set them aside to dry.

3. Stack and add brad

Stack the circles. Punch a small hole in the center of the stack using a Crop-A-Dile. Insert a brad to secure the flower.

Every Last Detail

Check upholstery stores for discontinued fabric samples. You can get them for free or at a discounted rate.

Felt Bloom

I love old-fashioned flowers, especially those fabric flowers on my grandmother's home décor pieces from the '50s—the ones made of thick felt and accented with silver glitter (my favorite!). I am always trying to figure out a way to duplicate a vintage look for projects such as this photo banner, and a felt bloom seemed like a good fit. Some felt and a hot glue gun are all that's really required to make them. Large blooms work well for home décor pieces like banners, but small flowers, made from smaller templates, are great for adding texture to layouts and cards.

family
happy
Other things may change us, but we start and end with the family.
~Anthony Brandt
When you look at your life, the greatest happinesses are family

Supplies: adhesive (iLoveToCreate); banner (Maya Road); chandelier crystals (Heidi Swapp); chipboard (Maya Road); decorative scissors (Fiskars); embossing powder (Ranger); felt (C.P.E.); flower stamens (Wilton); glitter glue (Ranger); ink (Clearsnap, Tsukineko); paper trim (Bethany Lowe); patterned paper (Jenni Bowlin); stamps (Cornish Heritage Farms); Misc: jump rings, pom-pom trim, yellow flower stamens, crackle medium, eyelets, acrylic paint, tags

What You'll Need

flower pattern (below), felt, fabric pen with disappearing ink, decorative fabric scissors with pinking edge, hot glue gun (or fabric glue), craft flower stamens, glitter glue

1. Cut out flowers

Copy and cut out the flower pattern (below). Then trace it onto felt five times using a disappearing ink fabric pen. Cut out the flowers using decorative scissors with pinking edges.

2. Attach first flower

Place one flower (Flower 1) flat onto your work surface. Add a dot of hot glue (or fabric glue) to the center of another flower (Flower 2) and fold it in half. Next, place a small dot of glue in the center of Flower 1 and attach folded Flower 2 over the left half of Flower 1.

(continued)

Flower Pattern

Copy this pattern at 100%. Cut it out to use it as the template for the five flowers. Photocopy the pattern at a smaller percentage to a make a smaller felt bloom.

3. Rotate, fold and attach second flower

Rotate the flower stack counterclockwise so that Flower 2 is on the lower half of the stack. Add a dot of glue to the center of a third flower (Flower 3) and fold it. Place another dot of glue on the center of Flower 1 and place folded Flower 3 on the left half of the stack (partially over the top of Flower 2). Your two folded flowers should form an L shape.

4. Add next flower

Turn your stack counterclockwise again. Fold another flower in half (Flower 4), adding a dot of glue to the center. Attach folded Flower 4 over the left half of the stack (as you did with Flower 3 in step 3), creating a new L shape.

5. Attach final flower

Fold the last flower (Flower 5) in half, adding a dot of glue to secure it. Pull back the upper half of Flower 4, and add a dot of glue to the center of the flower stack. Place Flower 5 at the upper half of the stack; the left side of Flower 5 should be under the upper half of Flower 4.

6. Gather and bend stamen

Gather several flower stamens. Bend the group in half so that all the ends are together.

Every Last Detail

You can find flower stamens in the baking section of craft stores.

7. Attach stamen to bloom

Add a good amount of glue to the bottom of the stamens and also the center of the flower stack. Push all the petals up toward the center and place the stamen in the center of the petals.

8. Accent edges

Accent the edges of the petals using glitter glue.

More Delightful Details

If you look closely, this paper flower might look similar to the felt flowers that adorn the banner. The difference is I created this flower on a smaller scale out of vintage book pages. I used a scallop punch to cut out the five flowers and assembled them as I did with the felt.

Supplies: ink (Clearsnap); patterned paper (My Mind's Eye); punch (Fiskars); rub-ons (Melissa Frances); vintage leaves (Paper Tales Inc.); Misc: thread, twine, book pages, floss, office tag, card

Machine Stitches

Using patterned papers with large prints can be intimidating. It's hard to know how to use a pattern like that without it overwhelming a project. I like to cut out patterns from these papers and use the details as custom embellishments. Here I cut out the word *beautiful*, which was the starting point for this page about my daughters. Compared to most of my projects, this layout has few details. Along with the paper and a bit of trim, machine stitches provide all the detail and texture needed to finish the page. A simple straight stitch dresses up the perimeter of the layout, while zigzag stitches connect the photos and block of paper for a quilted look. Just beautiful.

Supplies: letters, lace (Making Memories); Cluny lace (Wrights); decorative scissors (Fiskars); patterned paper (Webster's Pages); pom-pom trim (Maya Road); Misc: thread

What You'll Need

patterned paper, sewing machine, thread, adhesive

1. Sew a border

One option for sitching is to simply sew a border. Set your sewing machine to a straight stitch. Beginning in a bottom corner of your background, stitch around the perimeter, ¼" (6mm) to ⅛" (3mm) from the edge.

2. Stitch pieces together

Another stitching option is to "sew" two pieces of patterned paper together. Cut your pieces to size and attach them to the background. Then sew a zigzag stitch down the middle.

More Delightful Details

My favorite season, fall, and its first frost inspired this card. I love to see fall's warm color palette of dark orange, brown and red emerge after a hot and bright Texas summer. Some mornings, I even catch a twinkle of morning frost on pumpkins. For the base of this card, I used several patterned papers with similar fall tones. I accented elements using glitter and rhinestones to mimic the twinkle of that first frost. Simple straight stitches provide a bit of cozy texture.

Supplies: bling borders (Heidi Swapp); decorative scissors (Fiskars); glitter glue (Ranger); sticker (Melissa Frances); patterned paper, vintage transfers (Melissa Frances); Misc: brad, office tag, seam binding, card

Hand Embroidery

I wanted this album, featuring sepia-toned family photos, to have the feel of one created years ago that might have been stored in an old cedar chest. So I maintained a neutral, monochromatic color scheme in ivory, using products like felt, floss and old book pages. Timeless embroidery stitches make the perfect adornment for delicate felt flowers in the album's cover. Pearl bead accents provide beauty and charm.

Supplies: dies (Ellison); felt (C.P.E.); ink (Clearsnap); key, mini albums, scallop rickrack (Maya Road); metal frames (Junkitz); wax metallic finish (Amaco); Misc: embroidery floss, pen, thread, book page, metal heart, pearls, acrylic paint

Straight Stitch

French Knot

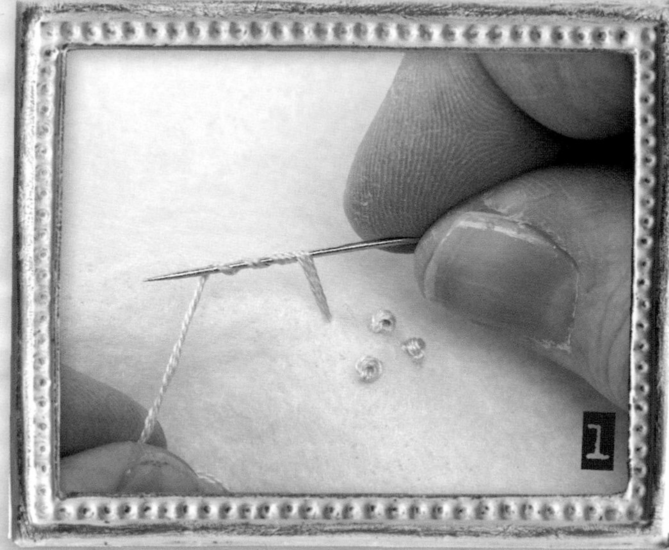

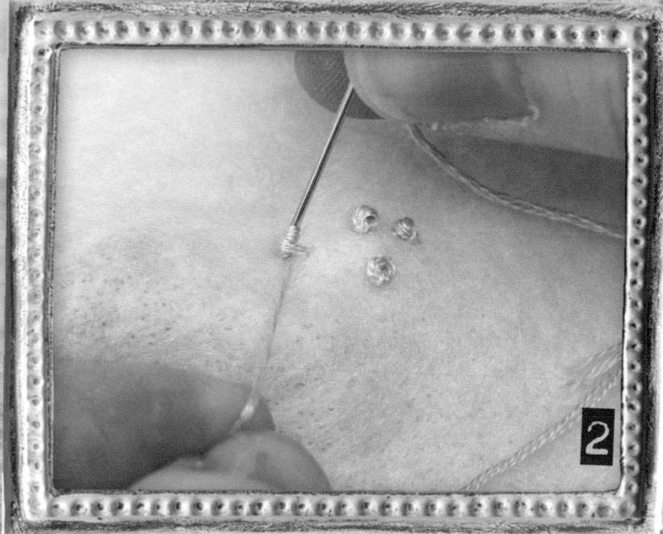

What You'll Need

felt, floss, needle, pearl bead, die-cut felt flower

Straight Stitch

Make a stitch

Thread the needle with three strands of floss and knot the end. Stitch a simple straight stitch in the center of each petal of the die-cut felt flower. To do so, insert the needle from the back of the felt to the front and then insert it.

French Knot

1. Wrap thread around needle

Thread the needle with three strands of floss and knot the end. Starting underneath the felt, bring the needle up through to the top. Make sure to hold the thread tight away from the felt and wrap the floss over and around the needle about four times.

2. Pull needle through

Holding the thread tightly, insert the needle next to the original hole and pull it through.

Every Last Detail

For a small French knot, wrap floss over and around the needle twice.

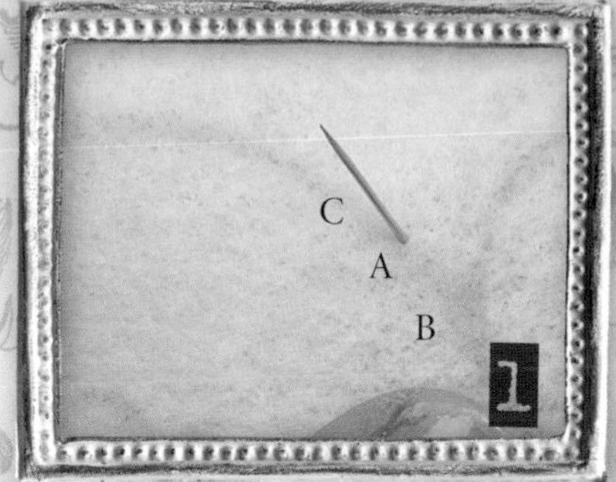

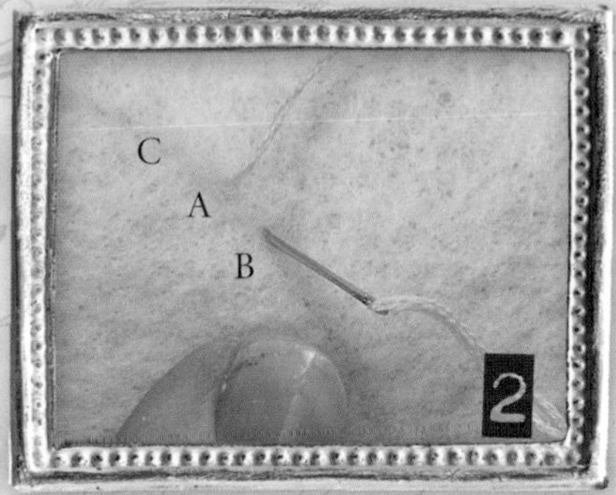

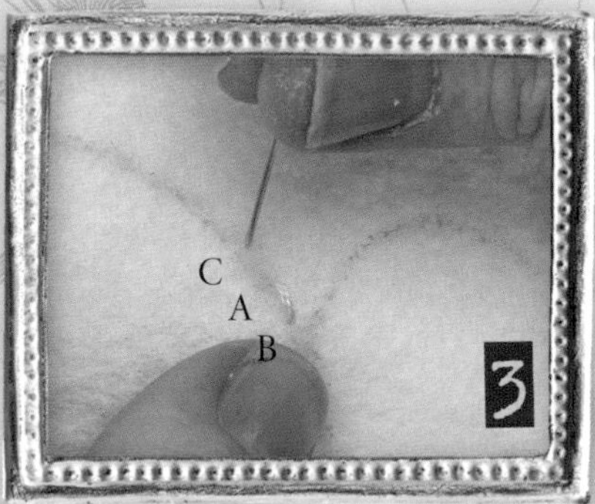

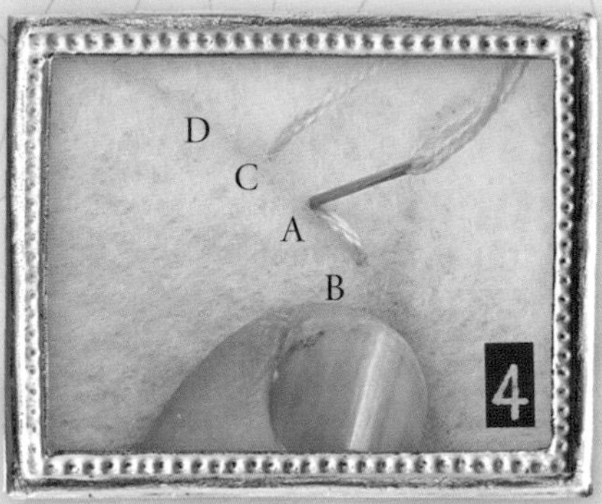

Backstitch

1. Insert through back of felt

Draw your pattern on felt using disappearing ink (I traced a chipboard scroll shape). Thread the needle with three strands of floss and knot the end. Starting from underneath your felt, bring the needle up through the felt (point A).

2. Insert needle into point B

Bring the needle back down through the felt at the next point (point B). The stitch should be about an ⅛" (3mm) wide.

3. Keep stitching

Come back up through the felt at point C (above point A), making sure your stitch is about ⅛" (3mm) wide.

4. Finish stitch

Insert the needle down into the felt at point A. To continue stitching, insert your needle up through the next point along the pattern line (point D), then insert it into point C. Continue along the pattern line. When you're finished, knot the floss underneath the felt.

More Delightful Details

This photo is one of my favorites of my aunt and uncle. I love that it shows the landscape, which was the inspiration for adding the daisies. I think they might have been blooming along the road during their day trip. The felt frame is a die-cut I hand-stitched using floss and a simple backstitch.

Supplies: canvas (Aaron Brothers); scroll, pins, blossom (Maya Road); die (Sizzix); glitter glue (Ranger); embossing folder (Provo Craft); ink (Clearsnap); patterned paper (Jenni Bowlin); pearl beads (Hobby Lobby); Misc: floss, thread, felt, silk flowers, tag, tulle, vintage cabochon, vintage seam binding, acrylic paint, eyelets

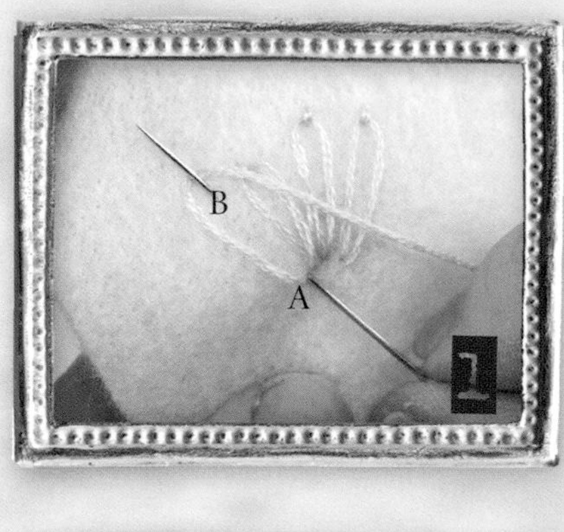

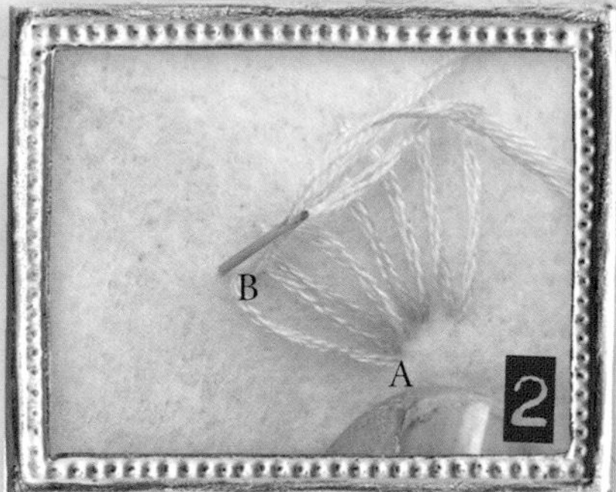

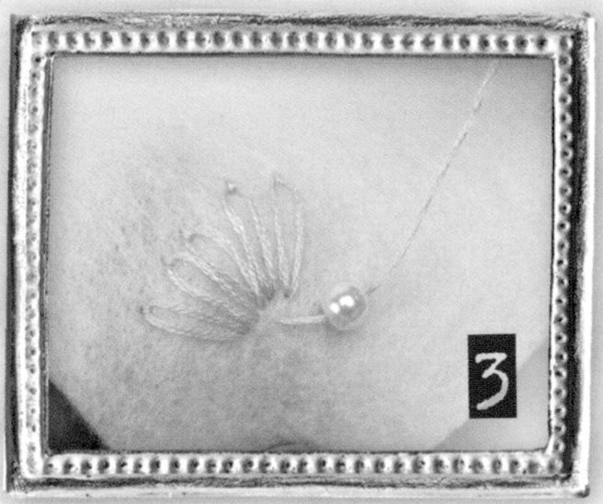

Daisy Stitch

1. Make loop

Thread your needle with three strands of floss and knot the end. Starting from under the felt, bring the needle up (point A). Then insert the needle very close to point A and bring it back up at the point where you want the top of the petal to be (point B). (The needle should still be inserted into both points A and B.) Wrap the floss behind the needle's tip (from left to right).

2. Secure loop

Pull the needle through the felt, creating a loop. Insert the needle into the felt, just above the loop (point B) to secure it. The tighter you pull the thread, the narrower the petal will be. Continue to add more petals.

3. Stitch on pearl

After you've stitched all your petals, bring your needle up through the center of the daisy. Thread your pearl on the floss.

4. Pull floss tight and knot

Insert the needle very close to the first hole, and pull tight. Secure with a knot underneath the felt.

More Delightful Details

I adore the simple loveliness of felt, especially when accented with delicate hand stitching. Embroidery takes the basic die-cut flowers on this tag to a whole new level. All it took to dress up the petals were a few stitches (straight stitch, backstitch and French knot). And a simple backstitch dresses up the butterflies, too.

Supplies: beads (Blue Moon Beads); chipboard scroll (Maya Road); decorative scissors (Fiskars); felt (C.P.E.); die-cuts (Sizzix); ink (Clearsnap); jewels (Creative Charms); twine (Beacon); Misc: office supply tag, vintage button eyelet, floss, wire

Embroidered Accent

Charm bracelets include a variety of shapes and styles in the charms, which is what I wanted to re-create on this layout about my mom as a young lady. I used several different items to embellish and accent the page. Pearls and rhinestones dress up the border, and delicate lace trim softens the edge. I chose two different patterned papers to create a quilted look and used shiny letters (covered in smoky quartz glitter) to balance the rhinestone border. Like a bracelet with beautiful charms, this embroidered leaf embellishment—which started from a stamped image—is adorned with beautiful rhinestone buttons to take center stage on the layout and highlight the theme.

This photo of Mom was taken when she was about
15 or 16 years old. To be honest the first thing
that catches my eye is the bracelet she is wearing.
I guess my love for bracelets
comes from Mom.
the bracelet

Supplies: bling borders (Advantus); letters (Maya Road); decorative scissors (Fiskars); felt (C.P.E.); ink (Clearsnap, Ranger); lace (Making Memories); patterned paper (Prima Marketing, Jenni Bowlin); pearls (Hobby Lobby); stamp (Studio 490/Stampers Anonymous); Misc: floss, glitter, thread, vintage rhinestone buttons, acrylic paint, photo corners

What You'll Need

felt, fluid chalk ink (in color similar to felt), stamp, scissors, needle, floss

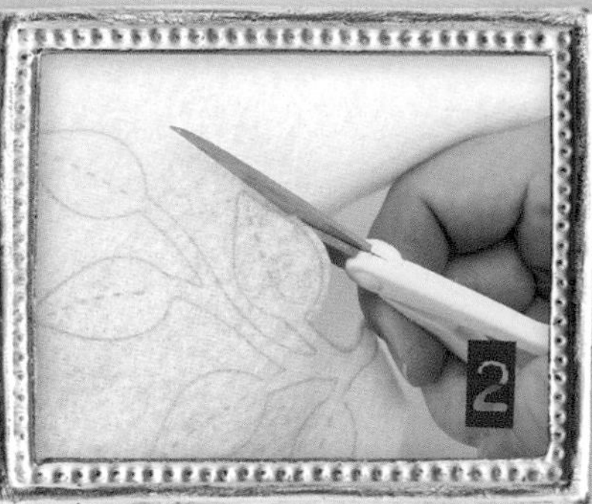

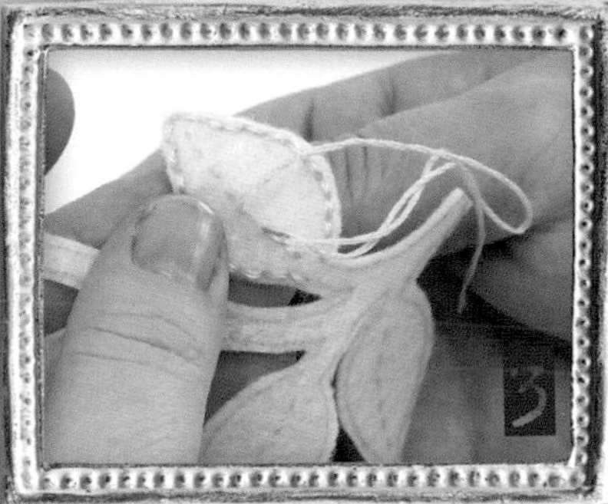

1. Stamp image

Ink your stamp using an ink color close to that of your felt. Stamp the image on the felt.

2. Cut out image

Cut out your stamped image, leaving at least a ⅛" (3mm) border.

3. Stitch with floss

Thread your needle with three strands of floss, and knot the end. Outline the stamp image using a backstitch.

More Delightful Details

I love all things homemade for Christmas, especially cards. To decorate this card, I stamped a tree image onto felt to act as my embroidery pattern, then stitched around the edge of the tree using a simple backstitch. I then stitched pearl beads onto the tree, accenting it with self-adhesive gold gems. Then I cut out the tree using micro-tip scissors, making sure not to get too close to my stitches.

Supplies: chipboard snowflakes (Maya Road); felt (C.P.E.); glass glitter (German Corner LLC); gems (Michaels); ink (Clearsnap, Ranger); pearls (Hobby Lobby); punch (EK Success, Fiskars); stamps (Studio 490/Stampers Anonymous); Misc: floss, twine, vintage sheet music, rhinestones, acrylic paint, card

IN A
FAR FAR away
Land
LIVED 2 sisters
I WILL be the gladdest thing
Under the sun!
I will touch a hundred flowers—
And not pick one.
I will look at cliffs and clouds
With quiet eyes,
Watch the wind blow down the
And the grass rise.
O WORLD, I cannot hold
close enough!
Thy winds, thy wide gray skies!
Thy mists that roll and rise!

Vintage Finds and Dimension

Sometimes it is all about the stuff. It's fun finding ways to incorporate little junk shop finds, vintage paper and dimensional items in your projects. Adding buttons, beads and vintage finds is an easy way to create details that pop. But making your own dimensional embellishments from simple supplies like ribbon and paper is also a fun way to make projects that stand out. In this chapter, you'll make the most of paper punches to create your own embellishments like the paper brooch on page 96. Check out page 104 to find out how to dress up plain white ribbon, and see how pipe cleaners can look elegant on page 112. You'll find the secret to creating perfect paper rosettes on page 102, and page 116 pulls several objects together to create a one-of-a-kind album cover. You never know what you'll find in a thrift shop, but one thing you can be sure of is that anything can add charming detail to a project.

Supplies: buttons (Autumn Leaves, My Mind's Eye); chipboard (Maya Road); decorative scissors (Fiskars); ink (Clearsnap); patterned paper (Sassafras); glitter glue (Ranger); leaves (Prima); letters (Advantus, Making Memories); Misc: baker's twine, floss, glitter, thread, book pages, pom-pom trim, stamens, vintage seam binding, acrylic paint

Acrylic Embellishments

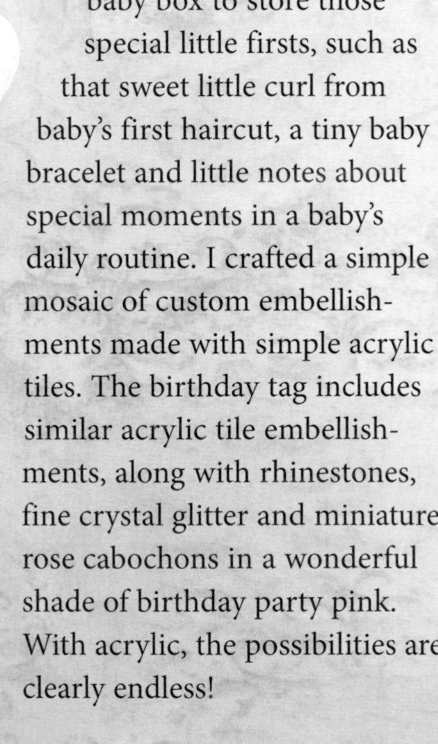

When you have a little one around, there always seems to be one thing or another that you want to keep, so you can never have too many keepsake boxes. And boxes also make great gifts for friends and family. I created this adorable baby box to store those special little firsts, such as that sweet little curl from baby's first haircut, a tiny baby bracelet and little notes about special moments in a baby's daily routine. I crafted a simple mosaic of custom embellishments made with simple acrylic tiles. The birthday tag includes similar acrylic tile embellishments, along with rhinestones, fine crystal glitter and miniature rose cabochons in a wonderful shade of birthday party pink. With acrylic, the possibilities are clearly endless!

Supplies (box): bling borders, acrylic tiles (Advantus); box, buttons, vintage sequin trim (Maya Road); stickers, patterned paper, vintage embellishments, vintage transfers (Melissa Frances); dimensional gloss medium, glitter glue (Ranger); ink (Clearsnap); Misc: twine, vintage seam binding, acrylic paint

Supplies (tag): crown, vintage sequins trim (Maya Road); stickers, patterned paper, vintage transfers (Melissa Frances); eyelet (Jo-Ann); acrylic tiles (Advantus); glossy accents, glitter glue (Ranger); Misc: glitter, thread, twine, Cluny lace, flowers, vintage seam binding, rhinestones

What You'll Need

patterned paper, rub-on, rub-on tool, small acrylic tile (like Fragments), dimensional gloss medium, scissors

1. Apply rub-on and gloss medium

Apply rub-on to patterned paper. Then cover one side of the acrylic tile with dimensional gloss medium.

2. Place tile and trim

Place the tile over the rub-on. Press the tile with a slight circular motion to help remove any air bubbles in the gloss medium. Once it's dry, trim off the excess patterned paper.

More Delightful Details

Old postcards are great for cards—tattered or pristine, it doesn't matter to me. This Christmas postcard had tattered edges, but the image was still beautifully intact. So I used portions of it to create acrylic embellishments delivering a holiday greeting. To add more dimension to the acrylic tiles, I wrapped baker's twine around the grouping several times and tied a bow at the base.

Supplies: acrylic tiles (Tim Holtz); decorative scissors (Fiskars); dimensional gloss medium (Ranger); glass glitter (German Corner LLC); patterned paper (DCVW); pearl gem (The Paper Studio); tinsel (Bethany Lowe); Misc: berries, book page, fabric, leaves, vintage postcard, vintage seam binding, card

Paper Brooch

Simple paper brooches add vintage charm to cards and tags, especially when coupled with lovely vintage-inspired patterned paper and rhinestone gems. This card has three times the charm! With coordinating punches, paper brooches are super simple to make. You can top off the brooch with faux vintage embellishments like these black-and-white cameos, or dig through your stash of gems and other vintage goodies. Add ribbon and a lacy scallop trim to a brooch-topped greeting card, and you're sure to send a sweet hello.

Supplies: ink (Ranger); patterned paper (Close to My Heart); pin (Maya Road); punch (EK Success); stamp (Cornish Heritage Farms); Misc: thread, corsage pin, lace, ribbon, vintage cameos, vintage button

What You'll Need

oval punches in two sizes, cardstock, patterned paper, adhesive foam, cameo or other oval-shaped vintage embellishment, strong liquid adhesive

1. Punch oval shapes

Use the larger punch to cut an oval from the solid cardstock. Then use the smaller punch to cut an oval from the patterned paper.

2. Layer oval shapes

Place adhesive foam in the center of the solid cardstock. Then attach the small oval on top.

3. Attach embellishment

Attach a cameo, gem or other oval vintage emebellishment using strong liquid adhesive (like hot glue) to the top of the oval stack.

Every Last Detail

You can accent the scallop edge on a paper brooch by adding rhinestones to the centers of each scallop or by poking a small hole with a paper piercer in the centers to resemble a small eyelet pattern.

Found Object Layers

Bits and pieces of vintage finds—no matter how small or worn—can make for a simply stunning piece. I created this Mother's Day tag by layering found objects, vintage pieces and dimensional details. Vintage ledger paper dresses the front of a large office tag, allowing the bird cut from a tattered postcard to take center stage. I used fabric strips cut with pinking shears to dress up the top of the tag. And the nest is filled with small feathers, tiny flocked flowers and rhinestone buttons to represent the bird's eggs.

Happy

Mothers

Day

Every Last Detail

Don't worry if the vintage postcard you love is torn, as long as a good portion of the image is still intact.

Supplies: bird nest (Hobby Lobby); decorative scissors (Fiskars); ink (Clearsnap); twine (Beacon); Misc: Cluny lace, fabric, feathers, vintage flowers, vintage ledger paper, vintage postcard, vintage rhinestones, thread, tag

What You'll Need

vintage paper, office tag, adhesive, scissors, postcard with image of bird, craft knife, craft mat, lace, baker's twine, needle, fabric glue, faux nest and feathers, tiny flowers, spherical buttons, hot glue gun

1. Adhere paper

Adhere the vintage paper to the office tag and trim off the excess. Then run the scissors' blade along the edge of the tag to distress it.

2. Cut postcard

Cut the bird from the postcard using a craft knife. Don't worry about the postcard's sentiment—you'll discard it. Attach the bird to the vintage paper.

3. Loop twine in lace

Cut a piece of lace to the width of the tag. Then thread a needle with baker's twine and loop the twine through the lace's holes. Attach the lace to the tag using fabric glue.

4. Build nest

Fill the nest with feather pieces, tiny flowers and spherical buttons. Attach the nest to the top of the tag using hot glue. Then punch a hole at the top of the tag, insert an eyelet and tie on fabric scraps.

More Delightful Details

This card shows another way to layer a vintage image with other found objects and dimensional details. Try punching circles from sheets of music, and layering vintage buttons and trim. Then sew a running stitch through felt using baker's twine.

Supplies: die-cut (Imagine That! Designs); felt (C.P.E.); ink (Clearsnap, Ranger); glitter glue (Ranger); jeweler's tag (American Tag Co.); leaf pins (Maya Road); pearl (The Paper Studio); stamp (Melissa Frances); vintage (Paper Tales Inc.); Misc: floss, punch, twine, fabric, sheet music, card

Simple Shaker Box

The inspiration for this tag—complete with a little shaker box filled with tiny beads—was a trip to an antique store, in which I found a bunch of old photo negatives. I thought the negatives would look lovely stitched onto a project, but I wished the photos were of my own family. I left the negatives behind, but when I got home, I printed a black-and-white photo of myself as a little girl onto a transparency to re-create the look. Patterned paper peeks out from behind the transparent image, which forms the shaker box. Seed beads bouncing in the box bring the photo to life. This simple shaker box adds interesting dimension and provides a sweet look that matches the smile on my face.

Her world was fresh and new and beautiful, full of wonder and excitement.

Every Last Detail

Transparencies are also great for making unique dimensional embellishments. Add rub-ons to a transparency, trim around the edges of the design and adhere to a project with dimensional adhesive dots. Add a button on top to hide the adhesive.

Supplies: buttons (Melissa Frances); chandelier crystals (Darice); decorative scissors (Fiskars); flower (Maya Road); ink (Clearsnap); patterned paper (Making Memories, Prima); rhinestone charm (Gartner Studios); ribbon (May Arts); transparency (DCWV); Misc: vintage beads, vintage seam binding, eyelets, floss, tag, thread

What You'll Need

black-and-white digital photo, transparency sheet, scissors, patterned paper, sewing machine, thread, seed beads

1. Print transparency

Print a black-and-white photo onto a transparency sheet, and cut it out.

2. Sew transparency to paper

Using a sewing machine, stitch three sides of the transparency to patterned paper. Make sure the pattern does not distract from important areas of the photo, such as a face.

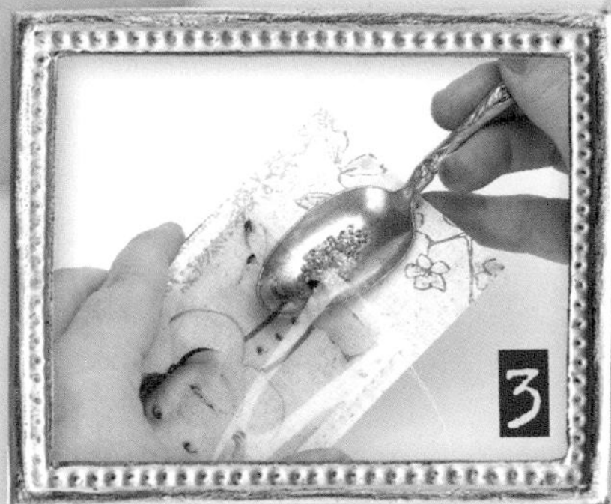

3. Add beads and close

Add seed beeds in a variety of colors to the newly created pocket. Stitch the remaining side closed.

More Delightful Details

To enhance the mystique of garden fairies, I printed these photos on transparencies. The barely there photo makes you ask, "Am I really seeing these little things?" I strategically placed the transparency images on the patterned paper so that it looks as though you are peeking in on a fairy through the foliage in her garden.

Supplies: album, rub-ons, pom-pom trim (Maya Road); bling borders (Heidi Swapp); glitter glue (Ranger); ink (Clearsnap); patterned paper (Making Memories, Prima); transparency (Die Cuts With A View); twine (Beacon); Misc: flowers, seam binding, stick pins, thread, rhinestones, wire

Paper Rosette

Paper rosettes add wonderful dimension to any project, and topped with vintage finds, they're even more charming. Plus, they're simple to make and require only two materials every paper crafter has on hand—paper and glue! Go simple with just a single rosette, or for gorgeous impact, try a garden of flocked rosettes to highlight heritage photos as I did. This circular layout with layer upon layer of texture—fancy trim, machine stitching, a paper doily, satin photo corners and sparkling letters—demanded over-the-top embellishments. The paper rosettes deliver, especially those accented with silver glitter glue. The black and red and all the sparkle highlight the photos beautifully.

Every Last Detail

You can vary the width of a rosette by changing the width of your paper strip (but keep it 12" [30cm] long). The diameter of a rosette is twice the width of the paper strip.

Supplies: chipboard letters (Maya Road); lace (Jo-Ann); brads, patterned paper (Little Yellow Bicycle); glass glitter (German Corner LLC); glitter glue (Ranger); Misc: floss, office tags, paper lace hearts, tulle, vintage rhinestone buttons, acrylic paint, photo corners, eyelets, crepe paper

What You'll Need

patterned paper, scoring tool, strong liquid adhesive, binder clip (optional), vintage find, glitter glue (optional)

1. Score paper

Cut a strip of patterned paper 1" × 12" (3cm × 30cm). Then score the paper strip every ½" (1cm).

2. Fold paper

Fold along the score lines in an accordion fashion.

3. Attach ends

Bring together the ends of the accordion-folded paper and attach using strong liquid adhesive (like hot glue). Hold the ends together (or add a binder clip to hold) while drying. Add a small amount of adhesive to the back of the rosette to secure it.

4. Add vintage find

Add adhesive to the front of the rosette, and attach a vintage find, such as a rhinestone button. Add glitter glue to the edges of the rosette, if desired.

More Delightful Details

Wanting to keep with the heritage theme of this baby photo, I accented the crackle frame with a simple paper rosette created from an old book page. Instead of meeting the ends, I folded the rosette only halfway to fashion a fan. To make your own, apply a strong liquid adhesive to the back of the fan and attach it to the frame. Hold the fan in place until the glue begins to hold, then attach the chipboard glittered heart on top of the fan with the strong adhesive.

Supplies: bell (Darice); chipboard heart, scroll frame (Maya Road); (DecoArt); glass glitter (German Corner LLC); ink (Clearsnap); glitter glue (Ranger); Misc: twine, book page, jump rings, vintage seam binding, acrylic paint, crackle medium

Painted Ribbon Bloom

I tend to stick to warm pastel shades in my work and let the glitter do all the attention-grabbing duties. But sometimes a project calls for a little color—and I sure do love to play with product! Dye-based mist (like Maya Mist) will transform plain ol' ribbon into a pretty canvas for a speckled pattern, which you can use to fashion a dimensional flower that will bloom on a project. A few vintage finds add nice detail to the top of the flower. The bloom on this layout demands attention, so I coupled it with transparent letters painted lightly with alcohol ink. Theirs is a soft, subtle look to balance the bold flower and also allow the patterned paper to show through.

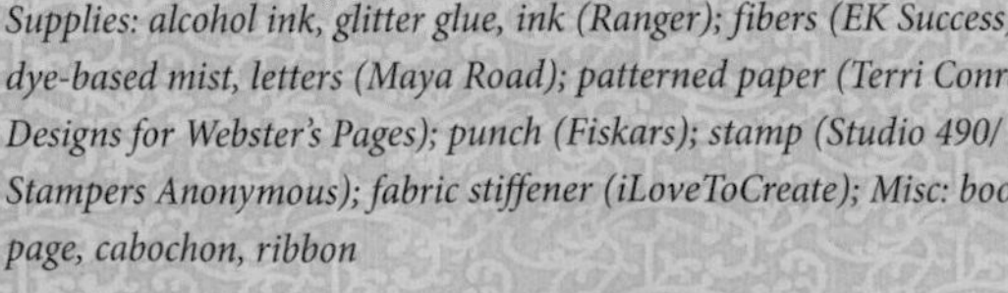

Supplies: alcohol ink, glitter glue, ink (Ranger); fibers (EK Success); dye-based mist, letters (Maya Road); patterned paper (Terri Conrad Designs for Webster's Pages); punch (Fiskars); stamp (Studio 490/ Stampers Anonymous); fabric stiffener (iLoveToCreate); Misc: book page, cabochon, ribbon

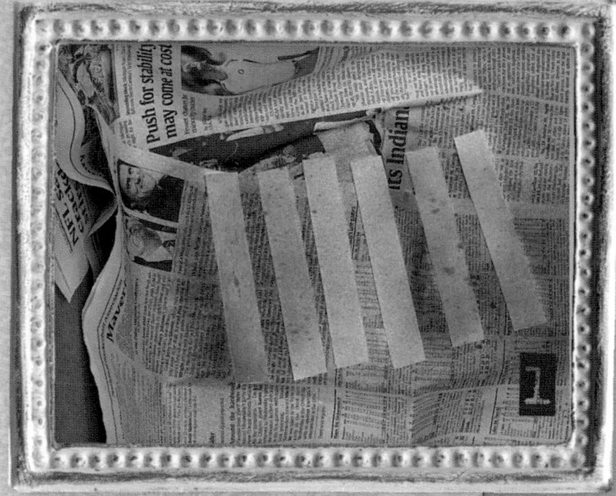

What You'll Need

white cotton ribbon (33" [99cm]), scissors, dye-based mist (like Maya Mist) in a color and in gold, cardboard box, newspaper, stamp, archival ink, adhesive, Crop-A-Dile, brad, scallop circle punch, book page, fiber, pearl, liquid glue

1. Cut and spray ribbon

Cut six strips of ribbon to 5½" (14cm). Place the strips in a box lined with newspaper, and spray with a dye-based mist. Then add a second coat of mist in gold. Once the ribbon dries, repeat on the back side.

2. Stamp ribbon

After the ribbon dries, stamp a pattern onto the top side of the ribbon using archival ink.

3. Stack three strips

Place three strips of ribbon face down on your work surface. Layer two of the strips in a cross shape and one strip down the center.

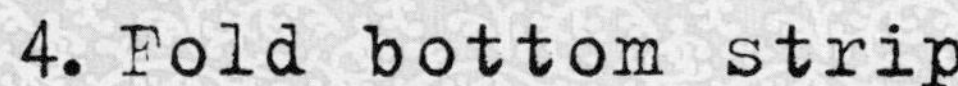

4. Fold bottom strip

Fold the end of the botton strip toward the center, and secure with a dot of adhesive.

(continued)

Every Last Detail

When using dye-based mists, another option for easy clean up is to line your kitchen sink with paper towels, place your ribbons on top and spray.

5. Fold remaining strips and repeat

Fold the next strip (in the middle layer) toward the center and secure. Then fold the strip on top and secure it. You should now have a flower with six "petals." Repeat steps 3-5 to create another flower.

6. Stack flowers and insert brad

Stack the two flowers, staggering the placement of the petals. Punch a hole in the center using a Crop-A-Dile and insert a brad to secure the stack.

7. Punch circle and roll fiber

Using a round scallop circle punch, cut a circle from an old book page and set it aside. Roll a small length of fiber into a spiral.

8. Attach circle, fiber and pearl

Attach the scallop circle to the flower on top of the brad using liquid glue. Then attach the fiber and a pearl.

Finding Vintage Goodies

Vintage finds are great to use in any project; they add detail and charm, texture and sheen, and of course, dimension. I have stores of old buttons, flocked flowers, postcards, tickets and other ephemera, seam binding and textiles, old sheet music and books, broken rosary beads, mismatched earrings and so much more!

Thrift stores are your easiest and best bet for everyday items like buttons, books and fabric. Also check garage sales and flea markets, as well as antique stores. Web sites like eBay (www.ebay.com) and Etsy (www.etsy.com) are also good places to scour for vintage objects, books, ledger paper and other supplies. In fact, I get all my baker's twine on eBay. And look beyond the obvious for goodies. Check out the clothing section of thrift stores for old rhinestone and pearl buttons you can snip off. Most of the time, the price for the entire article of clothing is less expensive than new button packs. Vintage pillowcases, sheets and blouses make for great fabric. Try wallpaper remnants in place of patterned paper.

Even if you have a hard time locating actual vintage goodies (or simply hate the hunt), you can easily fake the look. Vintage-inspired embellishments and papers are popular, so check your local scrapbooking store for faux finds. The baking section at craft stores is also a good place to look; you'll find a variety of small objects (meant as cake decorations) that look vintage.

More Delightful Details

Dye-based mist is great for ribbon, but it makes for beautiful accents made from a variety of materials. For this card, I crafted a delicate paper flower from vintage book pages and sewing patterns. To create a similar flower, punch two book pages in different sizes and trim with glitter. Then fold a section of sewing pattern so you will get three layers when cut. Using decorative scissors with pinking edges, cut one circle slightly smaller than the large book page circle and one circle slightly smaller than the smaller book page circle. Spray each circle (six total) with the mist. Crinkle the circles and, once everything is dry, layer the circles.

Supplies: chalk ink (Pebbles Inc.); glass glitter (German Corner LLC); glitter glue (Ranger); ink (Clearsnap); vintage newspaper (Kenner Road); dye-based mist (Maya Road); patterned paper (My Mind's Eye); punch (Fiskars); rub-ons (Melissa Frances); tag (Fancy Pants Designs); vintage leaves (Paper Tales Inc.); Misc: thread, sewing pattern, tag, vintage rhinestone button, card, eyelet

Vintage Paper Leaves

Vintage paper is one of my most favorite found objects for dressing up projects. Like patterned paper, it's versatile and easy to work with and alter. On this oversized tag, vintage paper leaves—cut from an old music sheet—add sweet detail and a bit of texture and vintage charm. Vintage paper actually makes an appearance all over this project—on the painted background, the flowers and the banner, too. I created the background by tearing a book page into several strips attaching them over the background with watered-down acrylic paint. I punched circles from another book page and painted those as well, then accented them with coarse glitter. The bases of the flower blooms are made from more paper—sheet music to match the leaves—while additional petals are cut from sewing patterns.

Supplies: buttons (Maya Road); decorative scissors (Fiskars); die (Sizzix); ink (Clearsnap); pearl beads (Hobby Lobby); pearl gems (The Paper Studio); ribbon (Imagine That! Designs, Inc.); Misc: floss, glitter, punch, sketch pencil, book page, fabric, office tag, trim, sewing pattern, acrylic paint, eyelets, decoupage medium

What You'll Need

vintage paper, decorative scissors with pinking edges, neutral-colored fluid chalk ink, sewing machine or needle, thread

1. Cut leaf

Cut a leaf from the paper using pinking scissors. If you are not comfortable cutting a leaf freehand, trace one onto the back of the paper and use it as your guide.

2. Ink leaf

Ink the edges of the leaf with neutral-colored chalk ink.

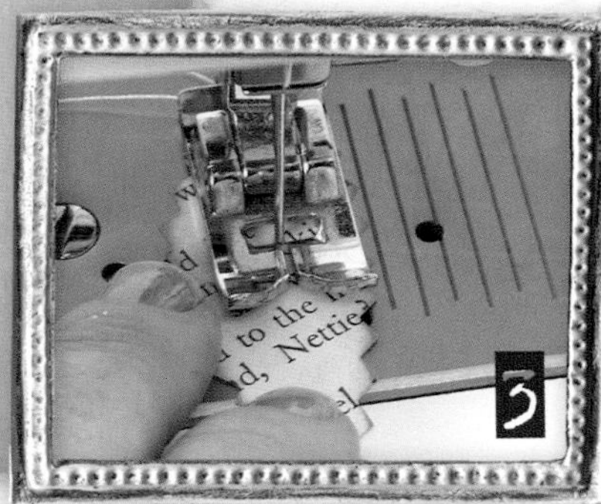

3. Stitch leaf

Stitch straight down the center of the leaf. You can either use a sewing machine or hand stitch.

More Delightful Details

Along with vintage music sheets, try old book pages, ledger paper or maps to craft some leaves. On this layout, little book page leaves add vintage charm to an otherwise modern layout. To add dimension to your leaves, bend each one upward as I did here.

Supplies: chipboard, velvet (Maya Road); die-cuts (Crate Paper); glitter glue (Ranger); ink (Clearsnap); letters (Adornit); patterned paper (Crate Paper, My Mind's Eye); Misc: thread, twine, book page, button, rhinestones, acrylic paint, crackle medium

Book Page Flower

This adorable vintage-inspired patterned paper reminds me of my childhood. I recall playing with my friends on the playground, promising each other we would be friends forever. The old-fashioned feel of the paper's design gave me the idea to use old newspaper pieces for the background and vintage book pages to create flowers. Book page flowers—which don't require any special tools to make—are subtle and simple, but they provide fabulous dimension for a project. I used book pages, but you can transform any thin paper into these blooms. For even more detail, the butterflies and chipboard scallops are accented with small pearls.

Every Last Detail

If you have a large scallop circle punch on hand, you can skip the folding and go on to step 4 (on the opposite page).

Supplies: chipboard banner, letters (Maya Road); decorative scissors (Fiskars); glass glitter (German Corner LLC); ink (Clearsnap); patterned paper (Marks Paper Company); pearl gems (Michaels, The Paper Studio); stamen (Wilton); vintage leaves, vintage necklace (Paper Tales Inc.); vintage newspaper (Kenner Road); Misc: punch, thread, twine, book page, chandelier piece, jump rings, rosary beads, vintage seam binding, acrylic paint

What You'll Need

book page, sharp scissors, liquid adhesive, flower stamen

1. Cut squares and fold

Cut three 3" (8cm) squares from the book page. Stack them and then fold in half to form a triangle.

2. Continue folding

Fold in half twice more. Then hold the triangle so the longest edge is on the left and the fold is at the right. Fold the right corner toward the long edge.

3. Cut folded squares

Cut off about ¾" (19mm) of the top of the triangle. Cut a semicircle.

4. Cut on fold lines

Unfold the triangle. Cut along each of the fold lines a little more than halfway toward the center.

5. Add stamen

Add liquid adhesive to the center of each flower and stack them. Then attach the folded stamen to the center. Separate and gather the petals around the stamen.

More Delightful Details

You can make smaller (or larger) book page flowers by varying the size of the squares. The smaller the square, the harder it is to fold, so don't go too small! For this elegant card, I used 2" (5cm) squares to create the flowers.

Supplies: bird (Heidi Swapp); chipboard (Maya Road); decorative scissors, punch (Fiskars); patterned paper (DoodleBug); flower stamens (Wilton); letters (Making Memories); Misc: card, acrylic paint, thread, book pages, glitter, vintage seam binding, thread, sewing pattern, tag, vintage rhinestone button, card, eyelet

Pipe Cleaner Vine

At times, I find patterned papers with large designs hard to use. Yet I always seem to find myself purchasing them because, well, I really like them! So what I do is use my craft knife to cut out the images just as I did in this layout. I loved this unique paper embossed with gold-foil details—one with a beautiful pattern and the other with soaring birds—so I cut out the designs and used them as a border to outline the page and as embellishments. Gold metallic pipe cleaners can easily scream tacky, but used in the right way, they can provide elegant detail for a project. On this layout, the pipe cleaner vine, complete with tiny blossoms and elegant blooms, perfectly complements the hand-cut gold details.

Supplies: chipboard (Maya Road); decorative scissors (Provo Craft); flowers, patterned paper (Fiskars); pearls (K&Co.); punch (EK Success); twine (Beacon); Misc: book pages, office tag, eyelet, glitter, rhinestone, acrylic paint, pipe cleaner, thread

What You'll Need

metallic pipe cleaner, chipboard scroll (optional), scissors, silk flower, decoupage medium, paintbrush, silk flower, glitter, vintage paper, scallop circle punch, pearl, vintage blossoms, strong liquid adhesive, tweezers (optional)

1. Shape pipe cleaner

Form the pipe cleaner into a scroll shape. If desired, use a chipboard scroll as a guide. Attach small pieces of pipe cleaner to the "vine" to make branches.

2. Add glitter

Brush decoupage medium on the silk flower. Then sprinkle glitter over the top and shake off the excess. Allow it to dry.

3. Cut paper flower

Using a scallop circle punch, cut a circle out of a piece of vintage paper. Cut petals into the circle.

4. Attach flowers

Layer the paper flower over the silk flower and attach a pearl. Create more flowers as desired. Add flower and vintage blossoms along the length of the vine using strong liquid adhesive (like hot glue).

More Delightful Details

Simple book page blossoms adorn the pipe cleaner vine on my "I Do" layout. But simple blooms can be used in so many ways. Here I used a die-cut machine to cut blossoms from book pages (along with felt and tulle), and gathered them to form a pretty lilac bloom accented with pearls.

Supplies: punches (Fiskars); die (Sizzix); felt (C.P.E.); ink (Clearsnap, Ranger); pins (Maya Road); patterned paper (My Mind's Eye); chalk ink (Pebbles Ink); pearls (The Paper Studio); stamp (Cornish Heritage Farms); Misc: thread, twine, book page, button, fabric, tulle, vintage seam binding

Button Bouquet

The starting point for this layout about my beautiful niece was my grandmother's quilt, which is shown in the lower portion of the photo. I pieced swatches of patterned papers together with a machine-sewn zigzag stitch. I wanted this layout to have a softness that included simple classic items like buttons, book pages, ribbon, trim and lace. A bouquet crafted from buttons and wire pops off the page and adds a happy, lighthearted touch. With the variety of buttons available, you can craft a button bouquet to suit any project—from a delicate bud made from vintage ivory buttons to a colorful bouquet like the one I made here. Glittered-edged leaves and simple book page blooms fill out the delightful bouquet and add rich texture to the project.

Every Last Detail

When hand-sewing a backstitch, first pre-punch the design using a paper piercer. This helps keep your stitches evenly spaced and speeds up the stitching process.

Supplies: buttons (Autumn Leaves, Heidi Grace); decorative scissors (Fiskars); jewels (Doodlebug); patterned paper (Jenni Bowlin); pearls (K&Co., Mark Richards); trim (BasicGrey, Making Memories, Wrights); glitter glue (Ranger); Misc: floss, punches, thread, twine, book page, crepe paper, wire

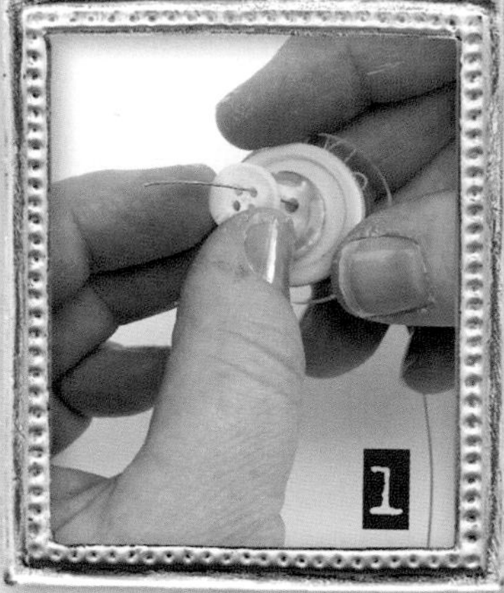

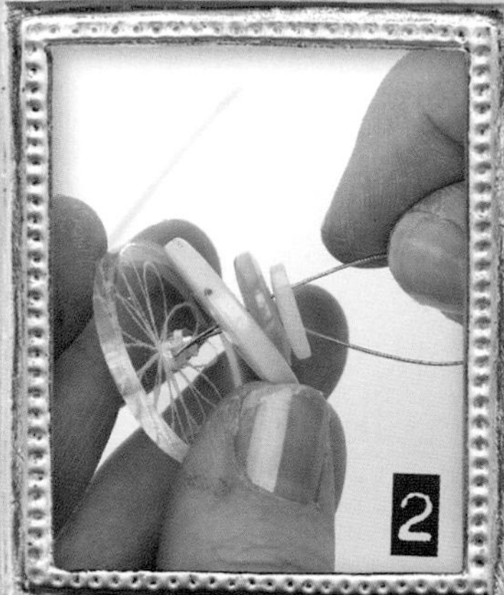

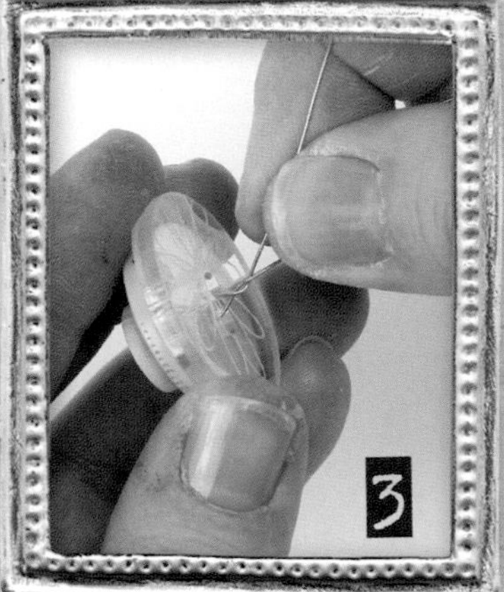

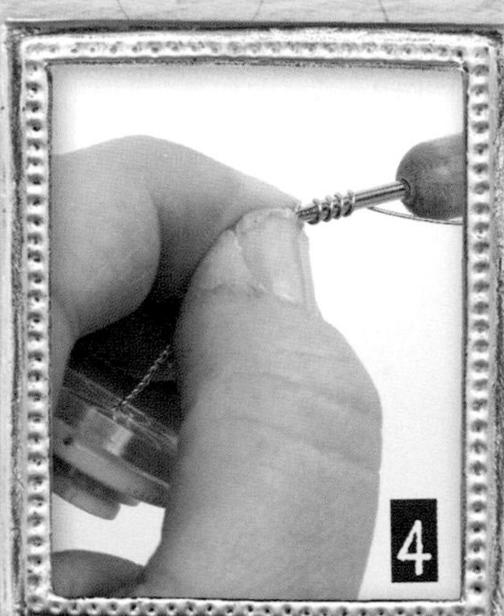

What You'll Need

24-gauge wire, wire cutters, 3–4 buttons, stylus

1. Add buttons to wire

Cut a piece of wire about 8" (20cm) long. Add a stack of buttons onto the wire.

2. Thread wire through buttons

Pull the wire through the buttons. Insert the wire back through the buttons using different holes.

3. Secure ends

Twist the ends of the wire at the back of the buttons to secure.

4. Curl wires

About 1½" (4cm) from the base of the buttons, wrap the wire several times around a stylus tip. Remove the stylus, and pull the wire to lengthen the curl.

Childers Family Picnic 1958

More Delightful Details

Button bouquets are bright and cheery, but they don't have to be made of buttons. On this patriotic tag, glittery chipboard stars stand in for buttons on the wire stems. The wire helps the stars pop out, mimicking fireworks, which is perfect for a Fourth of July photo. And lucky for me, lots of silver sparkle is the perfect accent for a Fourth of July display.

Supplies: crepe paper ribbon (Jenni Bowlin); decorative scissors (Fiskars); glass glitter (German Corner LLC); patterned paper (Graphic 45); stars, velvet, rickrack (Maya Road); Misc: glitter, thread, twine, vintage seam binding, acrylic paint, wire, crackle medium, crepe paper, eyelet

Candy Box Album Cover

Old-fashioned heart-shaped candy boxes inspired this dimensional mini album cover. I wanted the album to resemble an empty candy box holding treasured mementos. Topped with layers of paper, gold ribbon and found objects, the cover is just perfect! The inside pages are like the valentine holders I made in grade school, with pockets that allowed me to tuck photos of my grandparents and a copy of a letter my grandfather wrote to my grandmother when they were dating in 1926. The letter started with "My Dearest Girly" and ended with "P.S. Wrote with a hug, sealed with a kiss. I love the one that opens this. XOXO." Such sweet words from such a sweet and special man.

Supplies: chipboard album, pins (Maya Road); decorative scissors (Fiskars); doves (Wilton); glass glitter (German Corner LLC); glitter glue (Ranger); ink (Clearsnap); metal tag (Making Memories); patterned paper (The Paper Studio); ribbon (Jo-Ann, Offray); tissue garland (Bethany Lowe); Misc: glitter, thread, twine, lace, paper flowers, resin hearts, ribbon, acrylic paint

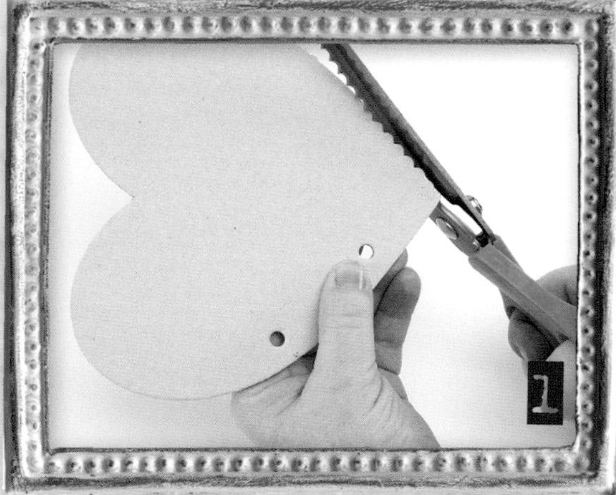

What You'll Need

chipboard heart album, heavy-duty decorative scissors with scallops, red acrylic paint, paintbrush, vintage-inspired patterned paper, pencil, scissors or craft knife, adhesive, decoupage medium, coarse glitter, small chipboard heart, tissue garland, wide white ribbon, thin gold ribbon, stapler, strong liquid adhesive, valentine-inspired objects (hearts, roses, doves, etc.)

1. Cut edge of cover

Using heavy-duty decorative scissors with a scallop edge, cut around the edge of the heart-shaped album cover.

2. Paint cover

Brush red acrylic paint on the album cover. Make sure the edges are completely painted. Allow the paint to dry. Then paint the back of the cover.

3. Cut patterned paper and attach

Using one of the inside pages as a template, trace a heart onto the patterned paper. Cut out the heart about a ¼" (6mm) inside the line. Adhere the heart to the painted album cover.

4. Add glitter to cover

Brush decoupage medium over the cover. Sprinkle a generous amount of coarse glitter over the decoupage medium. Shake off the excess glitter, and allow the cover to dry.

(continued)

5. Cut patterned paper for small heart

Cut a piece of the patterned paper to fit the top of a small chipboard heart (about 1" [3cm] smaller than the album cover). I used a heart-shaped coaster, but you could use a small album page or cut a heart from scrap chipboard.

6. Attach paper and tissue garland

Adhere the patterned paper to the front of the small chipboard heart. Then attach tissue garland around the edge of the heart.

7. Cut ribbon and create loops

Cut forty pieces of ribbon about 2" (5cm) long. Cut twenty pieces from a wide white ribbon and twenty from a thin gold ribbon. Layer a wide piece and a thin piece of ribbon and then fold them in half. Staple the ends to secure the loop.

8. Attach first ribbon loop

Attach the first loop to the back of the small heart using strong liquid adhesive (like hot glue). Most of the loop should hang off the edge. Attach two more ribbon loops to the back of the heart on either side of the first loop. They should overlap it.

9. Add rest of loops

Attach the next loop to the back, placing it slightly underneath the loop already attached. Attach the next loop slightly over the top. Continue attaching all 20 loops in the same manner until the edges of the heart are completly covered.

10. Add valentine objects

Attach the small heart to the top of the album cover. Then add a variety of valentine-inspired objects, like a big red bow, white doves, plastic valentines and red roses.

More Delightful Details

The interior pages are made from solid cardstock and patterned paper. To create the pages, I traced the back cover of the album onto scrap paper to make a template from which I cut three heart-shaped pages. To make the pockets, I cut two cardstock hearts in half horizontally and discarded the tops. Using a small amount of liquid glue on the two sides of the cut heart, I attached it to a cardstock page. I set two eyelets into each page using a Crop-A-Dile. To mimic the bottom of a candy box, I painted the back cover of the album metallic gold.

It's in the Details

Not too long ago I received a gift from a friend. I was just as excited with the way she wrapped my gift as I was to receive it! I was inspired to create this project with a mini album tucked inside the most adorable gift box. I sculpted the snowman from Styrofoam and various details in winter whites: white embellishments, iridescent glitter, clear glass shards, rhinestones and beautiful patterned papers. This set the tone for the winter-themed mini album that hides inside.

Supplies: air-dry clay (Creative Paperclay Co.); bling borders (Heidi Swapp); box, mini album, snowflake (Maya Road); decorative scissors (Fiskars); flower (Prima); glitter dust (FloraCraft) ; glitter glue (Ranger); ink (Clearsnap); paint (Making Memories) ; patterned paper (Heidi Grace); pom-pom trim (Hobby Lobby); rhinestone (Darice); twine (Beacon); Misc: brads, glitter, pom-pom trim, vintage mica, vintage seam binding, vintage sheet music, floss, thread, pipe cleaner, bell, decoupage medium

With so many friends and family having little bundles of joy lately I decided to create a card accented wih rhinestones, lace and pale pink … To me this is 100% baby girl. A simple bow tied from vintage pale pink seam binding attached to cream Cluny lace accents a bouquet of pale pink posies perfectly. The frame distressed with wax metallic finish highlights the lovely little bouquet. The rhinestones add a sparkling finishing touch.

Supplies: bling borders (Advantus); ink (Clearsnap); journaling page (Making Memories); wax metallic finish (Amaco); vintage frame (Melissa Frances); Misc: thread, twine, book page, Cluny lace, vintage flowers, vintage seam binding, card

I often use pieces of bracelets and necklaces as part of my wall hangings and ornaments. I found this beautiful pearl necklace in a thrift shop, left alone because it was broken, and grabbed it as fast as I could! The small colored pearls mix well with the other beads hanging below this ornament. To finish the beaded tassels, I added a small chandelier piece to the end of each strand.

Supplies: decorative scissors (Fiskars); glass glitter (German Corner LLC); jeweler's tag (American Tag Co.); scroll coaster, blossoms (Maya Road); vintage newspaper (Kenner Road); patterned paper (K&Co.); pearl gems (The Paper Studio); rhinestones (Darice); vintage beads, vintage leaves (Paper Tales Inc.); Misc: jump rings, chandelier pieces, trim, vintage necklace, eyelets

Placing handmade items around the house is a simple way to create a warm and inviting atmosphere. I like to display items like this one on black easels. You know that vintage paper makes simple floral accents. But you can create charming dimensional accents with vintage paper cut in varying shapes as well. For lovely embellishments like these, all you need are two paper punches of the same shape in different sizes. Punch three hearts from vintage paper and ink the edges of each. Then stack them, fold the sides up and stitch down the center.

Supplies: decorative scissors, punches (Fiskars); Dresden trim (German Corner LLC); felt (C.P.E.); ink (Clearsnap); pins (Maya Road); patterned paper (Jenni Bowlin, Making Memories); pearls (Michaels); Misc: thread, twine, office tag, seam binding, vintage buttons, vintage flowers, eyelet

For me, babies conjure images of soft pastels, tiny buttons and loads of love. My niece Isabella is the inspiration for this layout. After taking her newborn portrait, I crafted a layout using soft details and textures—like transparent accents, pretty scallop edges, simple stitching and tulle—that allow her photo to be the center of attention. Together the details add up to one gorgeous layout that helps the beautiful photo shine.

Supplies: buttons (Melissa Frances), chipboard letters, hearts (Heidi Swapp), decorative scissors (Fiskars), glitter glue (Ranger), ink (Clearsnap); patterned paper (BasicGrey); Making Memories); punch (EK Success); rub-ons (Daisy D's); pins (Heidi Grace); Misc: glitter, rhinestone, tulle, vintage flower, vintage seam binding, floss, tags, thread

I watched my niece get so excited over a birthday card with a coil-spring embellishment—she made it wiggle over and over again. So, I just had to re-create the look. On this card, a bright pink paper rosette topped with a vintage button provides dimension, while a ribbon stem and book page leaves supply texture. The butterfly provides an unexpected pop: It's attached to the card with a spring I created by coiling wire around the end of a stylus. When the recipient receives it, the butterfly will flutter just a bit … so easy and so fun!

Supplies: flocking powder (Hobby Lobby); bingo card (Jenni Bowlin); letters (Making Memories); patterned paper (My Little Yellow Bicycle); punch (Fiskars); tag (Junkitz); Misc: thread, book page, vintage rhinestone button, wire, eyelet

What's more perfect for a birthday celebration than a bright, cheery, sparkly birthday card? Here I topped a yummy cupcake with frosting made from hot pink glitter and a jewel. Next, I accented the patterned paper and crepe paper rosette with glitter glue. Finally, I added rhinestones and more jewels in spots around the card. To complete the project, I placed two jewel pins in the center of the bow.

Supplies: chipboard cupcake (Maya Road); decorative scissors, punch (Fiskars); glitter glue (Ranger); ink (Clearsnap); jewel flowers, pins (Maya Road); jeweler's tag (American Tag Co.); patterned paper (Making Memories, My Mind's Eye); rub-ons (Melissa Frances); gems (Michaels); Misc: glitter, twine, vintage seam binding, rhinestones, card, crepe paper

I have several special jewelry pieces I received from my grandmother and great-grandmother—such as my grandmother's cameo bracelet and faux pearl earrings and my great grandmother's black onyx ring and gold beaded necklace—that I've documented on this layout. To highlight these photos of beautiful vintage accessories, I added beautiful accessories of my own. A group of delicate crepe paper rosettes are paired with hand-stitched felt leaves. I tied office tags together with ribbon and twine to make a pretty canvas for my title and journaling.

Supplies: bling borders (Heidi Swapp); decorative scissors (Fiskars); glass glitter (German Corner LLC); glitter glue (Ranger); ink (Clearsnap); liquid embossing (Plaid); patterned paper (Creative Imaginations, Making Memories); pearls (Mark Richards); ribbon (Making Memories); rub-ons (Daisy D's); twine (Beacon); Misc: butterfly, fabric, felt, pom-pom trim, vintage seam binding, crepe paper, floss, office tags, acrylic paint, rhinestones, thread

I love to place projects in unexpected areas of my home for the seasons. These little ornaments are perfect to hang on cabinet knobs, in floral arrangements or on a spring-themed tree. Glitter plays a prominent role in this trio—coarse glitter and glitter glue dress up the frame, which borders vintage cutouts. I love accenting with both loose and liquid glitter in the same project. It provides a nice mix of shiny textures. The trick for the best and neatest application is to apply the loose glitter accents first. After I painted each of these chipboard frames (and let the paint dry), I applied a coat of decoupage medium and sprinkled on coarse glitter. Once the coarse glitter was dry, I accented the inner edges of the frames using silver glitter glue.

Supplies: buttons (Melissa Frances); scallop frames (Maya Road); ink (Clearsnap); glitter glue (Ranger); Victorian scraps (Victorian Scrapworks); vintage buttons (Paper Tales Inc.); Misc: glitter, twine, book page, chandelier pieces, acrylic paint

Sending handmade cards is a perfect way to keep in touch with all my craft-industry friends around the country. These plain silk blooms were in a pretty sorry state when I found them—overlooked and rather beat up. But I knew the little flowers would turn into a fabulous embellishment if I gave them a new life . To start, I detached the stems and layered the blossoms. I added glitter glue to some petals and coarse glitter to others. Once dry, I stacked the flowers and topped them with two pearl buttons tied together with baker's twine.

Supplies: crochet trim (Maya Road); gold pearls (Mark Richards); ink, glitter glue (Ranger); patterned paper (Cosmo Cricket, Jenni Bowlin); punch (Fiskars); stamp (Cornish Heritage Farms); vintage leaves (Paper Tales Inc.); Misc: floss, glitter, thread, silk flower, vintage button, card

With its vintage charm, crackle paint is a favorite wet medium of mine. It can mimic a variety of materials like bark on a branch or textured flower petals. Here I used it to give the illusion of feathers on the pastel birds. I applied a thicker layer of paint in some areas of each bird and a thinner layer in others so that the size of the cracks would vary. The birdcage sprinkled with shiny coarse glitter provides a nice contrast to the rough look of the painted birds.

Supplies: button (K&Co.); cage and bird, crochet trim (Maya Road); decorative scissors (Fiskars); distress crackle paint (Ranger); ink (Clearsnap, Ranger); journaling card (Imagine That! Designs); patterned paper (Making Memories, My Mind's Eye); pearl gems (The Paper Studio); stamp (Cornish Heritage Farms); Misc: glitter, thread, twine, leaf trim, vintage flowers, vintage seam binding, card

Each Christmas, I take photos of Ansley, and a cheery layout is a great way to show off those photos. With its shimmering quality that mimics the sun shining on a blanket of snow, glitter makes for the perfect accent for a winter-themed project. On this project, I accented some of the snowflakes on the patterned paper using glitter glue, then altered the chipboard letters and snowflake with glass shards and fine glitter. To bring focus to the photos, I placed a strip of rhinestones along the top and bottom of the photo group.

Supplies: bling borders (Advantus); chipboard letters, rickrack, snowflake (Maya Road); decorative scissors, punches (Fiskars); flocking (Hobby Lobby); glass glitter (German Corner LLC); patterned paper, stickers (October Afternoon); Misc: floss, glitter, acrylic paint, thread, button, pom-pom trim

Source Guide

The following companies manufacture products featured in this book. Please check your local retailers to find these materials, or go to a company's Web site for the latest product. In addition, we have made every attempt to properly credit the items mentioned in this book. We apologize to any company that we have listed incorrectly, and we would appreciate hearing from you.

7gypsies
(877) 749-7797
www.sevengypsies.com

Aaron Brothers
(972) 409-1300
www.aaronbrothers.com

Adornit/Carolee's Creations
(435) 563-1100
www.adornit.com

Advantus Corp.
(904) 482-0091
www.advantus.com

American Art Clay Co. (AMACO)
(800) 374-1600
www.amaco.com

American Crafts
(801) 226-0747
www.americancrafts.com

American Tag Company
(800) 223-3956
www.americantag.net

Art Institute Glitter, Inc.
(877) 909-0805
www.artglitter.com

Autumn Leaves
(800) 588-6707
www.autumnleaves.com

Avery Dennison Corporation
(800) 462-8379
www.avery.com

BasicGrey
(801) 544-1116
www.basicgrey.com

Beacon Adhesives, Inc.
(914) 699-3405
www.beaconcreates.com

Berwick Offray, LLC
(800) 237-9425
www.offray.com

Bethany Lowe Designs
(309) 944-6214
www.bethanylowe.com

Blue Moon Beads
(800) 377-6715
www.bluemoonbeads.com

Clearsnap, Inc.
(888) 448-4862
www.clearsnap.com

Close To My Heart
(888) 655-6552
www.closetomyheart.com

Cocoa Daisy
www.cocoadaisy.com

Cornish Heritage Farms
(877) 860-5328
www.cornishheritagefarms.com

Cosmo Cricket
(800) 852-8810
www.cosmocricket.com

CPE/Consumer Product Enterprises, Inc.
(800) 327-0059
www.cpesource.com

Crate Paper
(801) 798-8996
www.cratepaper.com

Creative Imaginations
(800) 942-6487
www.cigift.com

Creative Paperclay Company
(800) 899-5952
www.paperclay.com

Daisy D's Paper Company
(888) 601-8955
www.daisydspaper.com

Darice, Inc.
(866) 432-7423
www.darice.com

DecoArt Inc.
(800) 367-3047
www.decoart.com

Delta Creative, Inc.
(800) 423-4135
www.deltacreative.com

Déjà Views
(800) 243-0303
www.dejaviews.com

Dennecrepe Corporation
(978) 630-8669

Design Master
www.dmcolor.com

Die Cuts With A View
(801) 224-6766
www.diecutswithaview.com

DMC Corp.
(973) 589-0606
www.dmc-usa.com

DMD Paper
www.creativityinc.com/dmd

Doodlebug Design Inc.
(877) 800-9190
www.doodlebug.ws

EK Success, Ltd.
www.eksuccess.com

Ellison
(800) 253-2238
www.ellison.com

Fancy Pants Designs, LLC
(801) 779-3212
www.fancypantsdesigns.com

Fiskars, Inc.
(866) 348-5661
www.fiskars.com

Flora Craft
www.floracraft.com

Gartner Studios, Inc.
www.gartnerstudios.com

German Corner, LLC
(888) 393-0492
www.germanplaza.com

Graphic 45
(866) 573-4806
www.g45papers.com

Greg Markim, Inc.
(414) 347-9296

Hampton Art Stamps, Inc.
(800) 229-1019
www.hamptonart.com

Heidi Grace Designs, Inc.
(866) 347-5277
www.heidigrace.com

Heidi Swapp/Advantus Corporation
(904) 482-0092
www.heidiswapp.com

Hirschberg Schutz & Co., Inc.
(800) 221-8640

Hobby Lobby Stores, Inc.
www.hobbylobby.com

iLoveToCreate (a Duncan Enterprises Co.)
(800) 438-6226
www.duncanceramics.com

Imagination International
http://copicmarker.com

Imagine That! Designs, Inc.
No information

Jenni Bowlin
www.jennibowlin.com

Jo-Ann Stores
www.joann.com

Junkitz - no longer in business

K&Company
(888) 244-2083
www.kandcompany.com

Kenner Road
www.kennerroad.com

Krylon
(800) 457-9566
www.krylon.com

Li'l Davis Designs
(480) 223-0080
www.lildavisdesigns.com

Little Yellow Bicycle—see Déjà Views

Magic Scraps - no longer in business

Making Memories
(801) 294-0430
www.makingmemories.com

Mark Richards Enterprises, Inc.
(888) 901-0091
www.markrichardsusa.com

Marks Paper Company
www.markspaperco.com

Marvy Uchida/Uchida of America, Corp.
(800) 541-5877
www.uchida.com

May Arts
www.mayarts.com

Maya Road, LLC
(877) 427-7764
www.mayaroad.com

Melissa Frances/Heart & Home, Inc.
(905) 686-9031
www.melissafrances.com

Michaels Arts & Crafts
www.michaels.com

Mind's Eye, Inc.
(800) 665-5116
www.mymindseye.com

Novtex Corporation
(800) 227-1440
www.novtex.com

October Afternoon
www.octoberafternoon.com

Paper Studio
(480) 557-5700
www.paperstudio.com

Paper Tales Inc.
(586) 773-7911
www.papertales.com

Pebbles Inc.
(800) 438-8153
www.pebblesinc.com

Pink Paislee
(816) 729-6124
www.pinkpaislee.com

Pink Persimmon
www.pinkpersimmon.com

Plaid Enterprises, Inc.
(800) 842-4197
www.plaidonline.com

Prima Marketing, Inc.
(909) 627-5532
www.primamarketinginc.com

Provo Craft
(800) 937-7686
www.provocraft.com

Ranger Industries, Inc.
www.rangerink.com

Sassafras Lass
(801) 269-1331
www.sassafraslass.com

Scor-Pal
www.scor-pal.com

SEI, Inc.
(800) 333-3279
www.shopsei.com

Sizzix
(877) 355-4766
www.sizzix.com

Stampendous!
(800) 869-0474
www.stampendous.com

Stewart Superior Corporation
(800) 558-2875
www.stewartsuperior.com

Studio 490/Stampers Anonymous
www.stampersanonymous.com

Target
www.target.com

Terri Conrad Designs
www.terriconraddesigns.typepad.com

Tim Holtz
www.timholtz.com

Tsukineko, Inc.
(800) 769-6633
www.tsukineko.com

USArtQuest, Inc.
(517) 522-6225
www.usartquest.com

Victorian Scrapworks
www.victorianscrapworks.com/

Webster's Pages/Webster Fine Art Limited
(800) 543-6104
www.websterspages.com

Wilton Industries
(800) 794-5866
www.wilton.com

Wrights Ribbon Accents
(877) 597-4448
www.wrights.com

Index

Delight in your creativity with these other F+W Media books.

Pretty Little Felts

Julie Collings

Inside this playful book, you'll find more than 24 projects to tickle your fancy. *Pretty Little Felts* shows you how to combine all kinds of felt with unexpected mixed-media materials, including vintage fabric, paper, glitter, metal, beads, ribbon and wire. From useful pouches and needle books to delicate jewelry and whimsical ornaments and doodads, there's something here for every crafter.

ISBN-13: 978-1-60061-090-5
ISBN-10: 1-60061-090-0
paperback; 128 pages; Z1979

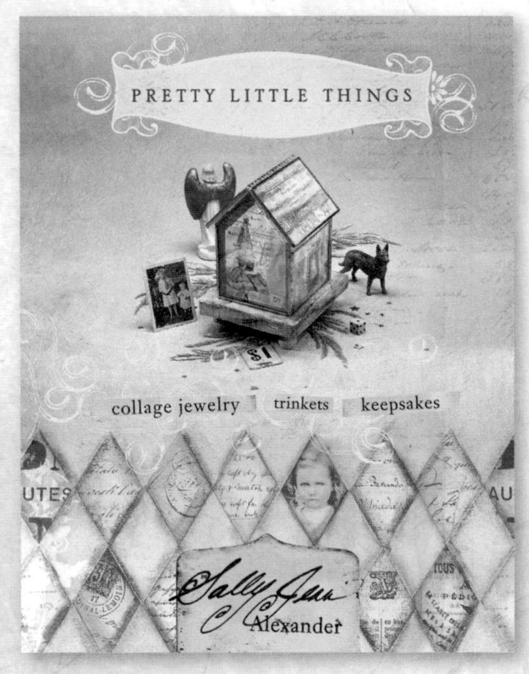

Pretty Little Things

Sally Jean Alexander

Learn how to use vintage ephemera, found objects, old photographs and scavenged text to make playful, pretty little things, including charms, vials, miniature shrines, reliquary boxes and much more. Sally Jean's easy and accessible soldering techniques for capturing collages within glass make for whimsical projects, and her all-around magical style makes this charming book a crafter's fairytale.

ISBN-13: 978-1-58180-842-1
ISBN-10: 1-58180-842-9
paperback; 128 pages; Z0012

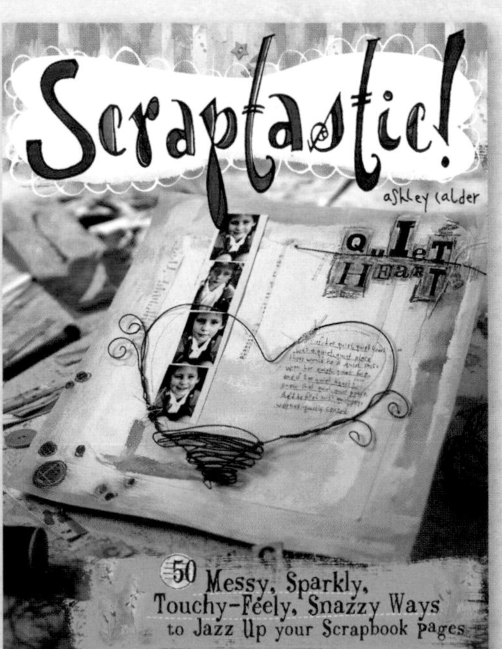

Scraptastic!

Ashley Calder

Get ready to infuse your scrapbook layouts with 50 messy, sparkly, snazzy and exciting new techniques. Go beyond the usual—experiment with art supplies, try unfamiliar tools, go wild and have fun. In Ashley Calder's debut book, she teaches you ways to take your projects to the next level using innovative ideas for creating playful and artistic pages.

ISBN-13: 978-1-59963-011-3;
ISBN-10: 1-59963-011-7
paperback; 128 pages; Z1007

These and other fine North Light and Memory Makers titles are available at your local craft retailer, bookstore or online supplier, or visit our Web site at www.mycraftivitystore.com.